Real Possibilities

Checklist *for* Family Caregivers

A Guide to Making It Manageable

Sally Balch Hurme

Defending Liberty
Pursuing Justice
AMERICAN BAR ASSOCIATION

Cover design by Jill Tedhams/ABA Publishing

The materials contained herein represent the opinions and views of the author and should not be construed to be the views or opinions of the companies with whom such person is associated with, or employed by, nor of the American Bar Association or the Senior Lawyers Division, unless adopted pursuant to the bylaws of the Association.

Nothing contained in this book is to be considered as the rendering of legal advice for specific cases. Readers are responsible for obtaining such advice from their own legal counsel or other professionals. This book and any forms and agreements herein are intended for educational and informational purposes only.

Limit of Liability/Disclaimer of Warranty: While the publisher, AARP, and the author have used their best efforts in preparing this book, they make no representations or warranties with respect to the accuracy or completeness of the contents of this book and specifically disclaim any implied warranties of merchantability or fitness for a particular purpose. No warranty may be created or extended by sales representatives or written sales materials. The advice and strategies contained herein may not be suitable for your situation. You should consult with a professional where appropriate. If professional assistance is required, the services of a competent professional person should be sought. The publisher, AARP, and the author shall not be liable for damages arising herefrom. The fact that an organization or website is referred to in this work as a citation and/or potential source of further information does not mean that the author, AARP, or the publisher endorse the information the organization or website may provide or recommendations it may make. Further readers should be aware the Internet websites listed in this work may have changed or disappeared between when this was written and when it is read.

19 18 17 16 15   5 4 3 2 1

Library of Congress Cataloging-in-Publication Data

The ABA/AARP checklist for family caregivers : a guide to making it manageable / edited by Sally Balch Hurme. — First Edition.
   pages cm
 Includes bibliographical references and index.
 ISBN 978-1-63425-151-8 (print : alk. paper)
1. Home care services—Law and legislation—United States—Popular works. 2. Older people—Home care—Law and legislation—United States—Popular works. 3. People with disabilities—Home care—Law and legislation—United States—Popular works. 4. Estate planning—United States—Popular works. 5. Caregivers—Legal status, laws, etc.—United States—Popular works. I. Hurme, Sally Balch, editor.
 KF3826.H64A72 2015
 649.8—dc23

2015014062

Discounts are available for books ordered in bulk. Special consideration is given to state bars, CLE programs, and other bar-related organizations. Inquire at Book Publishing, ABA Publishing, American Bar Association, 321 North Clark Street, Chicago, Illinois 60654.

AARP publishes a variety of books in print and electronic formats. Visit AARP.org/Bookstore.

www.ShopABA.org

Table of Contents

Chapter 7 Money Matters

Chapter 8 Retirement Plans and Investments

Chapter 9 Taking Care of Property

About the Author

Sally Balch Hurme, J.D.

Sally Balch Hurme, J.D., has led the national conversation on many of the legal issues of concern to older persons and their families. Whether the issue is how to make decisions for others, plan for what comes next, or avoid fraud, she's been in the forefront. Although she has written more than 20 law review articles on elder law topics, she has focused her professional career on explaining the law so everyone can understand it.

Hurme is quoted frequently in national media, including the *Wall Street Journal*, *USA Today*, the *New York Times*, *Money*, *Kiplinger's Retirement Report*, CNN.com, NPR, and Fox Business News. She is in demand as a speaker, having given more than 100 presentations on elder law topics in at least 40 states. She has lectured on elder abuse and guardianship in Australia, the Czech Republic, Germany, Great Britain, Italy, Japan, Moldova, the Netherlands, and Spain. *Checklist for Family Caregivers* is the third in the ABA/AARP Checklist series, which includes the best-selling *Checklist for Family Survivors*, *A Guide to Practical and Legal Matters When Someone You Love Dies*, and *Checklist for My Family*, *A Guide to My History, Financial Plans, and Final Wishes*.

Hurme started her legal career as a partner in a private law firm, gained valuable experience serving older clients as a legal services attorney, and served as a city magistrate in Alexandria, Virginia. She spent three years as an attorney adviser with the U.S. Department of Justice Office of Intelligence Policy and Review, working on counterterrorism and counterespionage cases. She then returned to elder law advocacy as an assistant staff attorney with the American Bar Association Commission on Law and Aging before moving to AARP. During her almost 25 years with AARP, she advocated on a wide range of issues, including consumer fraud, financial exploitation, elder abuse, surrogate decision making, advance care planning, predatory mortgage lending, health care fraud, and financial security. Hurme taught elder law as an adjunct professor at the George Washington University Law School for eight years, honing her ability to explain the law. She is a long-term member of the National Academy of Elder Law Attorneys, American Bar Association, and the Virginia and District of Columbia bars. Hurme was a member of the Discipline and Ethics Commission of the Certified Financial Planners Board of Standards. She is also vice-chair of the board of governors of the Stuart Hall School in Staunton, Virginia.

For the past two decades, Hurme's volunteer commitment has focused on the rights of adults with diminished capacity and the reform of guardianship policy and procedures. She has served multiple terms on the boards of the National Guardianship Association and the Center for Guardianship Certification, where she has been instrumental in developing standards for guardians and criteria to improve professional competency. She's been an adviser to the Uniform Law Commission in drafting the guardianship jurisdiction act and revising the uniform guardianship act. As chair of the National Guardianship Network, a collaboration of 11 national organizations working to improve guardianship, she led the planning for the 2014 World Congress on Adult Guardianship. As a member of the U.S. State Department delegation, she participated in the drafting of the Hague International Convention on the Protection of Incapacitated Adults. In 2008, she was honored by the National College of Probate Judges with the William Treat Award for excellence in probate law.

She received her B.A. from Newcomb College of Tulane University, New Orleans, Louisiana, and received her J.D. cum laude from the Washington College of Law, American University, Washington, D.C. She lives in Alexandria, Virginia, but enjoys getaway time at her farms near Shepherdstown, West Virginia, and Bridgewater, Virginia.

Introduction

You may not think of yourself as a caregiver, but if you help someone in your family with everyday tasks, the *ABA/AARP Checklist for Family Caregivers* is for you. You could be one of the 42 million family caregivers who provide unpaid help to someone they are close to who needs assistance. The person you care for could be your spouse, parent, sibling, adult child, or friend. Your caregiving may include driving to doctor's appointments periodically and grocery shopping each week. Or, you could help every day with bathing or getting dressed, preparing meals, and making sure medications are taken. You may be the one who steps up to pay the bills, locate legal documents, and track medical claims.

However much caregiving you provide, you have an abundance of important documents and information to keep track of. You need a way to understand and organize all the legal, financial, and medical matters pertaining to the person you care for. That's what this book helps you do. There are many excellent books that talk about caregiving with a personal touch, including my AARP colleague Amy Goyer's personal caregiving journey in the upcoming *ABA/AARP Juggling Life, Work, and Caregiving* (AARP.org/Caregiving Book). I add an organizational touch by helping you pull together the information you need to make your job easier, from listing medications to locating retirement savings to cover expenses. And I help you decipher some of the contracts you'll encounter and explain the ins and outs of making decisions for someone else.

In Chapter 1, you gather much of the basic information you need to know about those you care for, such as driver's license number and blood type, along with more personal information, such as what they care about and what they can do with and without help. Additionally, use the checklists to evaluate personal and financial safety: Is the person safe, prepared for emergencies, or at risk for scams or exploitation?

This job, as you've probably learned, is way too big to do by yourself. Chapter 2 is where you put contact information for those you know you can call in an emergency to help with caregiving responsibilities. Others on your caregiving team include service providers, medical professionals, financial advisers, and lawyers. Use the checklists to get their contact information in one place. You'll also find tips on questions to ask financial or legal professionals before hiring them. If the person you are caring for is a veteran, be sure to know all the support available to caregivers from the Department of Veterans Affairs (VA).

The Where to Find It Checklist is key to Chapter 3. It is where you keep track of important documents. Use this checklist to identify what information you should have and where you put it so you don't have to hunt for it when you need it. In this chapter, I also address access to safe deposit boxes, digital assets, and rewards programs.

In addition to being a caregiver, you may be called upon to carry out legal roles. Chapter 4 outlines the responsibilities of agents with a power of attorney, trustees, representative payees for Social Security, VA fiduciaries, and guardians. All people have the right to make their own decisions, and they also have the right to have someone else make decisions for them, if they wish. Powers of attorney are the most common legal documents used to give another the authority to make those decisions. Along with the authority comes much responsibility. Making decisions for another is not easy. To make decisions for another means you have to thoroughly understand what the person wants you to do. You have to put aside what you would do yourself. Chapter 4 explains what you need to know about these important responsibilities.

Most caregivers have to know a lot about medical care and the experts who provide that care. The checklists in Chapter 5 help you organize medical matters, track medications, understand how to be a health care agent, and recognize the difference between advance directives and medical orders such as do not resuscitate orders.

Chapter 6 helps you decipher some of the contracts you may encounter as you care for a family member. I help you know what to look for in contracts to hire care providers, through an agency or on your own. You'll find tips on how to understand resident agreements for both assisted living and skilled nursing care facilities. If the person you care for has a long-term care insurance policy or a pre-need funeral arrangement, you need to know what's in the contract so you can make sure to get all benefits that have been paid for. Family caregiver agreements are legally complicated but can be a way to pay family members who provide care. A lawyer's advice is important for all contracts.

Paying for care is a challenge for many families. Use the checklists in Chapter 7 to organize income and expenses and identify possible benefits that could augment resources. Are there personal loans on the positive side or outstanding debts on the negative side of the balance sheet? If so, record them on the checklists. Also include credit or debit card balances. Just as credit card accounts can be a source of funds as well as a debt that must be paid, a reverse mortgage can be a source of income as well as a debt to pay back. The checklists in this chapter provide a current financial picture to help create a budget.

Use Chapters 8 and 9 to list pension benefits, retirement plans, and investment accounts, along with inventories of real and personal property. As a financial manager, you need to know what resources are potentially available to pay for daily living expenses along with long-term care. Chapter 10 covers some of the insurance that protects the person you care for. Dealing with Medicare and other health insurance claims can be very daunting and time consuming. Use the resources in this chapter to navigate health coverage issues. One insurance tip: Make sure vehicle insurance covers other drivers.

In Chapter 11, the final chapter, you learn about how the person you care for wants his life celebrated when he dies. You can use this chapter to start the conversation about whether he wants to be an organ donor, where he's to be buried, and if he wants military honors at the grave site. Find out if he wants to create an ethical will to leave behind special words of guidance to later generations. Does he have a will? If he wants to create a will but hasn't done so yet, share the tips in Chapter 11 to start the process of creating an estate plan.

How to Use This Book

Each chapter starts with a My To-Do Checklist to help you get started collecting the information you need to gather about the person you care for. For each item on the checklist, you will find basic information about what you need and why as well as tips on how to locate and organize it. Use this section of each chapter to guide you through what you need to do. After the explanations, you'll find Action Checklists where you record the details you've gathered and what you have done.

You will probably want to start by looking through the My To-Do Checklists on pages xiii–xvi to get an overview of the many topics covered by this book. Go through a first run to check off the items that don't apply to the person you care for. You may find that you'll want to start with the sections or checklists that are easiest for you to accomplish. Check off each item on the My To-Do Checklist as you complete that step.

Don't try to complete this guide in one or two sittings. Approach it in manageable sections or add to it as you learn more about the person you care for. Even though you might not have all the answers at first, take the time to find them. You will find tips on how to gather some of the information and places to record your information on the Action Checklists.

Over time, you'll learn more about those you care for, their plans, what they want, and how they feel. Their circumstances, along with how they wish to be cared for, may change. Feel free to modify the checklists according to their needs. If there's a detail that doesn't apply, just skip it. You'll find plenty of spaces to record information; use as much as you need.

You should also prioritize: What should be completed sooner rather than later? Your priority list is unique, but you may want to put at the top of your list getting a complete list of medications, recording contact information for all the people you rely on, locating insurance policies, and indicating where important papers are located.

A few tips:

Fill in the paper checklists with a pencil or erasable pen. This book is made to be written in. As you gather more information as time goes by, it will be easy to update what you have previously written.

Download the electronic files from http://ambar.org/caregivers. As you complete a chapter, you may want to print out a copy and place the pages in a three-ring binder. You may also want to add plastic pages to slip in documents you come across. You'll want to keep a hard copy (and a backup file) of these documents in your filing system. Be sure to note where you have those copies stored so you don't waste time looking for them later.

Keep the information up to date. As changes occur, you'll want to note them. Set aside some time each month to review the checklists and add new information.

A word of caution: You are assembling a great deal of very personal information you don't want to get into the wrong hands. Be cautious about where you store it and with whom you share it.

My To-Do Checklists

I have completed the following To-Do Checklists:

What I Need to Know

- ❏ Gather details about the basics
- ❏ Talk about goals, needs, interests, likes, and dislikes
- ❏ Assess activity levels—what can be done with and without help
- ❏ Identify difficulties managing finances
- ❏ Know the signs of financial exploitation
- ❏ Make sure the residence is safe
- ❏ Prepare for an emergency
- ❏ Take care of myself

Our Caregiving Team

- ❏ Keep track of who on the caregiving team is doing what
- ❏ Know whom to call in an emergency
- ❏ List all who provide personal services
- ❏ List health professionals
- ❏ List financial professionals and know the different types available
- ❏ List legal professionals and know how to find them
- ❏ Check out help from your employer
- ❏ Take advantage of support available to veterans and their caregivers

Know Where It Is

❑ Locate important information and note where it is

❑ Shred papers that contain personal information

❑ Know how long to keep records

❑ Know where the safe deposit box is, what's in it, and who has access

❑ Keep track of online assets and keep them secure

❑ Check on rewards programs

Making Decisions for Another

❑ Know what it means to be an agent with a power of attorney

❑ Know what it means to be a trustee

❑ Know what it means to be a representative payee or VA fiduciary

❑ Know what it means to be a guardian

Medical Matters

❑ Compile a medical history

❑ Compile and carry a personal medication record

❑ Understand your role as a health care agent

❑ Understand any DNR or POLST in place

Deciphering Contracts

❑ Know what to include in a family caregiver agreement

❑ Consider whether to hire home care services directly or through an agency

❑ Be prepared to negotiate the contract if hiring home care services directly

❑ Make sure you understand the services included in a home care agency contract

❑ Understand what is and isn't provided in an assisted living facility contract

❑ Understand what is and isn't provided in a skilled nursing facility contract

❑ Learn to read the fine print in a long-term care insurance policy

❑ Know what has been paid for in pre-need funeral arrangements

Money Matters

- ❑ List all income and expenses
- ❑ Find out what's in the bank
- ❑ Understand Social Security benefits and how to navigate the system
- ❑ Check out veterans' benefits
- ❑ Get a copy of military service records
- ❑ Apply for other available public benefits
- ❑ Look for outstanding loans and debts
- ❑ Know how to deal with debt collectors
- ❑ Know how a reverse mortgage works

Retirement Plans and Investments

- ❑ Track down all pension benefits
- ❑ Document all retirement plans and understand the withdrawal rules
- ❑ Identify stocks, bonds, mutual funds, and other savings vehicles

Taking Care of Property

- ❑ List real property and review how it is titled
- ❑ Discuss with a tax adviser or estate planner the pros and cons of adding a child to a deed
- ❑ Determine if any property qualifies for tax relief
- ❑ Consolidate all investment or commercial property records
- ❑ Understand the terms of any rental agreements
- ❑ Obtain a copy of the master deed and condominium association documents
- ❑ Obtain and review any time-share contracts
- ❑ Inventory special personal possessions

Insurance Protection

❑ Review life insurance policies and know how they work

❑ Identify health insurance policies and know how they work

❑ Verify or obtain homeowner's or renter's insurance

❑ Verify and keep updated vehicle insurance

❑ Identify annuities and know how they work

Making Final Arrangements

❑ Confirm wishes regarding organ or body donation and autopsy

❑ Locate or support steps to create an ethical will

❑ Know wishes for the body

❑ Consider commemoration after death

❑ Plan for burial

❑ Check out burial benefits for veterans

❑ Locate or support steps to create a will

❑ Locate or support steps to create a letter of instruction

My Action Checklists

I have completed the following Action Checklists:

What I Need to Know

- ❑ Personal History
- ❑ Getting to the Heart of Things
- ❑ Activity Levels
- ❑ Signs of Difficulties Managing Finances
- ❑ Signs of Financial Exploitation
- ❑ Home Safety
- ❑ Emergency Preparedness
- ❑ Taking Care of Myself

Our Caregiving Team

- ❑ Team Tasks
- ❑ Backup Care/Emergency Contacts
- ❑ Care and Services Contacts
- ❑ Health Contacts
- ❑ Financial Contacts
- ❑ Legal Contacts
- ❑ Employer Leave Policies and Other Caregiver Supports
- ❑ Veteran's Caregiver Supports

Know Where It Is

❑ Where to Find It

❑ Safe Deposit Boxes

❑ Storage Units

❑ Digital Assets

❑ Rewards Programs for Airlines, Hotels, and Rental Cars

Making Decisions for Another

❑ Agent with a Power of Attorney

❑ Trustee

❑ Representative Payee/VA Fiduciary

❑ Guardian

Medical Matters

❑ Medical History

❑ Personal Medication Record

❑ Health Care Power of Attorney

❑ Medical Orders (Do Not Resuscitate/POLST)

Deciphering Contracts

❑ Family Caregiver Agreements

❑ Independent Home Care Contracts

❑ Agency Home Care Contracts

❑ Assisted Living Facility Contracts

❑ Skilled Nursing Facility Contracts

❑ Long-Term Care Insurance Policies

❑ Funeral Pre-Need Arrangements

Money Matters

- ❏ Income
- ❏ Bank Accounts
- ❏ Social Security Benefits
- ❏ Veterans' Benefits
- ❏ Public Benefits
- ❏ Expenses
- ❏ Credit and Debit Cards
- ❏ Lawsuits and Judgments
- ❏ Outstanding Loans
- ❏ Personal Debts
- ❏ Reverse Mortgage

Retirement Plans and Investments

- ❏ Pensions
- ❏ Retirement Plans
- ❏ Certificates of Deposit
- ❏ Money Market Funds
- ❏ Municipal Bonds
- ❏ Mutual Funds
- ❏ Savings Bonds
- ❏ Stocks and Bonds
- ❏ Treasury Bills, Notes, and Bonds

Taking Care of Property

❑ Commercial Property

❑ Condominium

❑ Investment Property

❑ Personal Property and Heirlooms

❑ Primary Residence

❑ Rental Residence

❑ Secondary Residence

❑ Time-Share

❑ Trust

Insurance Protection

❑ Health Insurance

❑ Homeowner's and Renter's Insurance

❑ Life Insurance

❑ Vehicle Insurance

❑ Annuities

Making Final Arrangements

- ❏ Final Wishes Summary
- ❏ Burial
- ❏ Celebration of Life
- ❏ Charities
- ❏ Cremation
- ❏ Entombment
- ❏ Ethical Will
- ❏ Funeral/Memorial Service
- ❏ Letter of Instruction
- ❏ Obituary
- ❏ Organ and Tissue Donation
- ❏ People to Contact
- ❏ Will and Codicil
- ❏ Veterans' Burial Benefits

PDF versions of these checklists can be found at http://ambar.org/caregivers.

CHAPTER 1
WHAT I NEED TO KNOW

You've probably already realized that as you carry out your caregiver responsibilities, you need a lot of pertinent information about the person you are caring for. Some information you already know and carry around in your head; maybe you've known each other your whole life and possibly even lived together for many years. But putting down in one place all those details makes it very handy for you to quickly access information when you need it.

You may need to dig around to find phone numbers for all the relatives or the blood type of the person you're caring for, but at some point in the future you'll be glad you did. I recently realized I didn't know my own blood type; I'll find out the next time I see my doctor so I can write it down in case my family needs it in an emergency.

In addition to those basic facts, you also need to be sure you understand who the person is, including strengths, wishes, and abilities. You might also want to take this opportunity to look at safety and security.

Finally, turn the spotlight around. To help another person, you'll need to first take care of yourself.

This chapter walks you through gathering all this preliminary information. As with all the chapters in this book, you'll first find the to-do checklists, with why and how to gather what you need. Then you'll find the action checklists, where you record what you know, have observed, have done, or need to do. If there's a detail that doesn't apply, just skip it. I've given you plenty of spaces to record information; use as much as you need.

My To-Do Checklist

Done	Need to Do	
❑	❑	Gather details about the basics
❑	❑	Talk about goals, needs, interests, likes, and dislikes
❑	❑	Assess activity levels—what can be done with and without help
❑	❑	Identify difficulties managing finances
❑	❑	Know the signs of financial exploitation
❑	❑	Make sure the residence is safe
❑	❑	Prepare for an emergency
❑	❑	Take care of myself

✓ Gather details about the basics

To get started, you can use the Personal History Checklist to record information you may be called upon to know. You'll want things like Social Security and driver's license numbers, which you'll need if a wallet is lost or stolen. If the person was in the U.S. military, you'll need to know the service serial number. I think I know my husband's serial number by heart, but I also have written it down just in case I forget it.

✓ Talk about goals, needs, interests, likes, and dislikes

Now let's move to the next step, the Getting to the Heart of Things Checklist, which is a lot more personal. Moving beyond names and numbers, you can use this checklist to jot down what you know about the person's heart and soul. What's important to him now and in the future? What are his talents, values, and goals? What does he really like? It could be lobster, the sunshine, or jazz music. Special dislikes might be cauliflower and not receiving thank-you notes. If you're not sure, take the time to find out. These conversations may not happen right away, but you do want to learn more to increase your awareness of what makes him happy, frustrated, content, or upset. You'll keep this information uppermost in mind as you make sure he receives the kind of care he wants and has the quality of life that's important to him.

✓ Assess activity levels—what can be done with and without help

You may be helping with just a few things like going to appointments or shopping for groceries, or you may be heavily involved in day-to-day activities. What you are doing now and what you may need to do in the future depend primarily on his needs. The Activities Checklist is a quick way to identify what he can do with no problems and what you need to help with.

At some point, he may need a more structured assessment of what he can do on a daily basis. This would be an assessment by a professional of activities of daily living, called ADLs:

- Feeding
- Toileting
- Selecting proper attire
- Grooming
- Maintaining continence
- Putting on clothes
- Bathing
- Walking and transferring (such as moving from bed to wheelchair)

The assessment would also include what are called instrumental activities of daily living (IADLs):

- Managing finances
- Handling transportation (driving or navigating public transit)
- Shopping
- Preparing meals
- Using the telephone and other communication devices
- Managing medications
- Performing housework and basic home maintenance

Doctors, rehabilitation specialists, and geriatric social workers are just a few of the professionals who can conduct these functional assessments.

✓ Identify difficulties managing finances

One area of concern may be around managing finances. The person you care for may have expressed frustration over, for example, deciphering medical bills or keeping track of what bills need to be paid.

To be sure, many of us share the same feeling from time to time. Some of us may never have been comfortable navigating financial waters and have gotten in over our heads with tricky transactions. I long ago gave up trying to reconcile my bank statement to the penny every month because the task caused more anxiety than reassurance about my bank balance.

The person you care for may just need some reassurance that he is managing money just fine. On the other hand, he may not be interested in your help and think he has no problems. You want to make sure there's no financial crisis such as overdue bills, a utility shutoff, or a foreclosure notice that could be avoided with some better organization or oversight. Use the Signs of Difficulties Managing Finances Checklist to be alert for indications that there might be problems taking care of money. If you are observing some problems, talk with him about what assistance he needs.

You can do a number of things to help with money management. You could sit down together to sort through the mail and explain bills or insurance claims. Together you can set up a filing system to match doctor bills with Medicare Summary Notices and put routine bills for utilities, cable, rent, or telephone on autopay to avoid writing checks every month. If you don't have the time or skill to do some of these things, he may want to engage a daily money manager to take care of these tasks. You can find a list of daily money managers at the American Association of Daily Money Managers, www.aadmm.com. Beyond these steps, he may want to give you the authority to be a financial agent by signing a financial power of attorney. Read about this in Chapter 4, Making Decisions for Someone Else.

✓ Know the signs of financial exploitation

Every day, hundreds of people—folks just like you and me—fall for scams. I know it all too well. My husband got a call one day from someone pretending to be our daughter, claiming to need $3,000 to get out of jail. With a well-rehearsed script and fancy acting, she convinced my husband to wire the money. Needless to say, our daughter was just fine, and the money was forever gone.

Scammers have dozens of tricks they use to con people out of their money. Most pitches have been around for decades, such as "Congratulations, you have won . . ." promising a fantastic sum of money if you'll just pay a fee to claim your winnings. Realistic-looking websites for fake charities raising money for disaster relief, starving children, and homeless dogs tug at heartstrings as they steal money. It's well known that consumers who fall for a scam or give to a fake website are bound to be contacted again and again.

You can be sure that my husband now is extremely alert and cautious about any questionable telephone call or email because I've made sure he knows about scammers' tactics. Unfortunately, too many people don't know that they've been scammed; if they did, the tricks wouldn't be so successful time and time again. You need to watch for the signs of scams, such as many calls from telemarketers, sweepstakes mail, or boxes of trinkets, greeting cards, or small prizes that can be part of a money-stealing gimmick.

Scammers' favorite weapons are the telephone, email, or mail, pretending to be their prey's best friend. On the other hand, people who exploit work behind closed doors because they most likely are the victim's friend or even a family member. Exploiters isolate potential victims by cutting them off from their usual social network, frequently by saying they, the exploiter, can be trusted more or love them more than others. To be successful, exploiters need to do two things: create a false sense of trust and do it in secret. By cultivating trust, they are able to convince their victim that they should be given access to the victim's money or property, use his automated teller machine (ATM) card, or be added to bank accounts, be deeded property, or be named in a will. They have to try to hide what they are doing from others—including the victim—or set up smoke screens of deception so that what they are doing won't be discovered. Use the Signs of Financial Exploitation Checklist to watch for these signs. Learn more about avoiding fraud at www.aarp.org/fraudwatchnetwork.

If the person you care for is in immediate danger, call 911. Report possible scam activity to the police, your state attorney general's office (www.naag.org at the Who's My AG? link), the Federal Trade Commission (www.ftc.gov/complaint), and the Consumer Financial Protection Bureau (www.cfpb.gov/complaint). Contact the local Adult Protective Services to report suspected elder abuse or financial exploitation. The elder care locator at www.eldercare.gov or 800-677-1116 can give you the local number to call. If your loved one is in a skilled nursing facility, the person to contact is the long-term care ombudsman. You can find the number to call at www.ltcombudsman.org.

✓ Make sure the residence is safe

You should also assess whether the current residence is safe. Just about all of us want to stay in our homes just as long as we can safely do so. AARP research consistently finds that the vast majority of people age 50 and older want to stay in their homes and communities for as long as possible. Some simple and often affordable changes—handrails, grab bars, night lights, and adjustable shower seats, to name a few—can make a home safer as well as more comfortable for people of all ages and abilities. Use the Home Safety Checklist in this chapter as you walk through rooms to spot safety hazards and reduce the chance for falls. For more detailed home safety checklists, tips on do-it-yourself fixes, and resources for improvements that may take a trained professional, use the AARP Home Fit Guide at www.aarp.org/homefit or see the *AARP Guide to Revitalizing Your Home*, available in bookstores.

✓ Prepare for an emergency

No matter where the person you care for lives, you want to make sure she is safe from natural disasters such as hurricanes, flooding, or fires. If she is in an assisted living facility or nursing home, check with the administrators to make sure they have in place carefully thought-out and practiced emergency evacuation procedures. If she lives on her own or with you, it's essential that you have an emergency evacuation plan and an emergency preparedness kit. Use the Emergency Preparedness Checklist, based on guidance from the Federal Emergency Management Agency (FEMA), to do both. Go over the plan together to make sure she can stay calm in any emergency and know what to do to be safe. Your plan should pay particular attention to any special needs, including an escape chair that can be used to get down stairs for someone who uses a wheelchair or walker, extra hearing aid batteries, food for a service dog, backup power for oxygen units, and copies of all drug prescriptions.

Before the emergency happens, find and review any insurance policies to see what would be covered in the case of a natural disaster (see Chapter 10). Go over the policy with the insurance agent. Don't wait until after the disaster; then it is too late to get needed coverage. Depending on where the home is located, flood insurance may not be available or covered only with special policies. The federal government offers National Flood Insurance for people who live in areas where flooding is common. You can get information about these policies at www.fema.gov/information-property-owners. Read FEMA's *Answers to Questions about the National Flood Insurance Program* that you can download at that same site.

✓ Take care of myself

Whether you are suddenly thrust into a caregiving role or gradually take on increasing responsibilities, it's crucial that you take the time to take care of yourself. As rewarding as caregiving can be, it can also be draining physically and emotionally. If you don't take care of yourself, you will not be as good at taking care of someone else as you could be. You need to understand the wide range of emotions that family caregivers feel, recognize how stress affects you, and plan how you'll manage to stay healthy. Are you getting enough sleep, eating a balanced diet, getting some exercise? Lack of sleep and poor nutrition are prime stepping-stones to overall poor health, lowered resistance to illnesses, and reduced energy. You know all that, but taking care of yourself can be challenging when your caregiving responsibilities are added to all the other things you do. Take a few minutes to go through the Taking Care of Myself Checklist to see how you are doing. Come back to this checklist frequently to note your progress in moving checks out of the "needs work" column.

What I Need to Know
Action Checklists

The following Action Checklists are included in Chapter 1:

❑ *Personal History*

❑ *Getting to the Heart of Things*

❑ *Activity Levels*

❑ *Signs of Difficulties Managing Finances*

❑ *Signs of Financial Exploitation*

❑ *Home Safety*

❑ *Emergency Preparedness*

❑ *Taking Care of Myself*

Personal History

Name: _____

                 First   *Middle*   *Last*

Name at birth: _____

                            First   *Middle*   *Last*

Place of birth: _____

                         City   *State*   *Country*

Date of birth: _____

Date of adoption: _____

Legal name change: _____

                           First   *Middle*   *Last*

Legal name change date: _____

Legal name change court: _____

                         Court   *City*   *State*

Current address: _____

_____

# of years: _____

Phone: _____ Cell phone: _____

Email: _____ Email: _____

Blood type: _____

Organ/tissue donor:

❏ Yes   ❏ No

Citizenship: _____

❏ By birth   ❏ By naturalization

Naturalization date: _____

Naturalization place: _____

                                City   *State*   *Country*

Military veteran:

❑   Yes

❑   No

Branch of service: _____

Dates of service: _____

Serial #: _____ Rank: _____

Type of discharge: _____

Social Security #: _____

Passport #: _____ Expiration: _____

Country of issue: _____

Driver's license #: _____ Expiration: _____

State identification card #: _____

State of issue: _____

Registered to vote at precinct: _____ County: _____ State: ___

Faith/Denomination: _____

Place of worship: _____

Address: _____

Pastor/Priest/Rabbi/Spiritual leader: _____

Phone #: _____

Email: _____

Marital Status:

❑   Divorced

❑   Married

❑   Never married

❑   Widowed

First spouse

Name of spouse: _____

Date of birth: _____

Place of birth: _____

Date of marriage: _____

Date of divorce: _____

Date of death: _____

Spouse is buried at: _____

Phone: _____ Email: _____

Address: _____

_____

Second spouse

Name of spouse: _____

Date of birth: _____

Place of birth: _____

Date of marriage: _____

Date of divorce: _____

Date of death: _____

Spouse is buried at: _____

Phone: _____Email: _____

Address: _____

_____

Children

Name of first child: _____

Phone: _____ Email: _____

Address: _____

_____

Name of spouse: _____

Phone: _____ Email: _____

Address: _____

_____

Name of grandchild: _____

Phone: _____ Email: _____

Address: _____

_____

Name of grandchild: _____

Phone: _____ Email: _____

Address: _____

_____

Name of grandchild: _____

Phone: _____ Email: _____

Address: _____

_____

Name of grandchild: _____

Phone: _____ Email: _____

Address: _____

_____

Name of second child: _____

Phone: _____ Email: _____

Address: _____

_____

Name of spouse: _____

Phone: _____ Email: _____

Address: _____

_____

© American Bar Association

Name of grandchild: _____

Phone: _____ Email: _____

Address: _____

_____

Name of grandchild: _____

Phone: _____ Email: _____

Address: _____

_____

Name of grandchild: _____

Phone: _____ Email: _____

Address: _____

_____

Name of grandchild: _____

Phone: _____ Email: _____

Address: _____

_____

Name of third child: _____

Phone: _____ Email: _____

Address: _____

_____

Name of spouse: _____

Phone: _____ Email: _____

Address: _____

_____

Name of grandchild: _____

Phone: _____ Email: _____

Address: _____

_____

Name of grandchild: _____

Phone: _____ Email: _____

Address: _____

_____

Name of grandchild: _____

Phone: _____ Email: _____

Address: _____

_____

Name of grandchild: _____

Phone: _____ Email: _____

Address: _____

_____

Name of fourth child: _____

Phone: _____ Email: _____

Address: _____

_____

Name of spouse: _____

Phone: _____ Email: _____

Address: _____

_____

Name of grandchild: _____

Phone: _____ Email: _____

Address: _____

_____

Name of grandchild: _____

Phone: _____ Email: _____

Address: _____

_____

Name of grandchild: _____

Phone: _____ Email: _____

Address: _____

_____

Name of grandchild: _____

Phone: _____Email: _____

Address: _____

_____

Getting to the Heart of Things

Personality:

_____

_____

_____

_____

_____

Values:

_____

_____

_____

_____

_____

Religious beliefs or practices:

_____

_____

_____

_____

_____

Skills and talents:

_____

_____

_____

_____

_____

Short-term goals:

_____

_____

_____

_____

_____

Long-term goals:

_____

_____

_____

_____

_____

Interests and activities:

_____

_____

_____

_____

_____

Special likes:

_____

_____

_____

_____

_____

Special dislikes:

_____

_____

_____

_____

_____

_____

Activity Levels

Activity	Can Do Independently	Needs Some Help	Needs Help
Get in and out of shower/tub			
Shave			
Wash hair			
Style hair			
Dress			
Brush teeth			
Trim fingernails			
Trim toenails			
Toilet			
Control bladder			
Manage incontinence			
Prepare meals			
Grocery shop			
Feed self			
Select appropriate foods			
Chew			
Swallow			
Make medical appointments			
Get to appointments			
Schedule tests			
Follow doctor's instructions			
Take medications on time/correct dosage			
React to an emergency			
Communicate needs			
Get into/out of a chair			
Get into/out of a bed			
Drive			

Activity	Can Do Independently	Needs Some Help	Needs Help
Use public transportation			
Do household chores			
Use checkbook			
Use ATM			
Manage personal expenses			
Manage investments			
Use telephone			
Use computer			
Use personal emergency response unit			
Take care of pets			
Stay safe from falls			

Signs of Difficulties Managing Finances

- ❑ I have observed the following difficulties managing finances:
    - ❑ Unopened mail
    - ❑ Late payment of bills
    - ❑ Repeat payments of bills
    - ❑ Unusual spending patterns
    - ❑ Mounting credit card debt
    - ❑ Calls from debt collection agencies
    - ❑ Utility shutoff
    - ❑ Foreclosure or eviction notice
    - ❑ Confusion about how to interpret an invoice, statement, or letter
    - ❑ Inability to write checks
    - ❑ Difficulty balancing checking account
    - ❑ Stress and confusion over paperwork
    - ❑ Disorganization of paperwork
    - ❑ Loss of ability to manage email or computer
    - ❑ Excessive telemarketing callers
    - ❑ Victimized by scammer
    - ❑ Multiple payments to charities
    - ❑ Trinkets and prizes
    - ❑ Sweepstakes mail

Signs of Financial Exploitation

❏ I have observed the following signs of possible financial exploitation:

❏ Excessive telemarketing callers

❏ Multiple payments to charities

❏ Significant change in spending pattern

❏ Unusual activity in bank accounts

❏ Financial transactions that can't be explained

❏ Use of credit card or ATM card by others

❏ Bank statements no longer being received

❏ Checks made out to cash

❏ Wire transfers to nonfamily members

❏ New "best friend"

❏ Exclusion from usual circle of friends or social activities

❏ Someone new making financial transactions or decisions

❏ Missing money or property

❏ Change in names on bank accounts, deeds

❏ Change in power of attorney or will

❏ Change in beneficiaries on life insurance, retirement accounts

❏ Suspicious signatures on checks or documents

Home Safety

Steps, Stairways, and Walkways

Yes	No	
❏	❏	Are they in good shape?
❏	❏	Do they have a smooth, safe surface?
❏	❏	Are there handrails on both sides of the stairway?
❏	❏	Are there light switches at the top and bottom of the stairs?
❏	❏	Is there grasping space for both knuckles and fingers on railings?
❏	❏	Are the stair treads deep enough for your whole foot?
❏	❏	Would a ramp be feasible in any of these areas if it became necessary?

Floor Surfaces

Yes	No	
❏	❏	Is the surface safe?
❏	❏	Is the surface nonslip?
❏	❏	Are there any throw rugs or doormats that might slip underfoot?
❏	❏	Is carpeting loose or torn?
❏	❏	Are there changes in floor levels?
❏	❏	If so, are they obvious or well marked?
❏	❏	Do you have to step over any electric, telephone, or extension cords?

Driveway and Garage

Yes	No	
❏	❏	Is there always space to park?
❏	❏	Is it convenient to the entrance?
❏	❏	Does the garage door open automatically?

Windows and Doors

Yes	No	
❏	❏	Are windows and doors easy to open and close?
❏	❏	Are locks sturdy and easy to operate?
❏	❏	Do doorways accommodate a walker or wheelchair?
❏	❏	Can you walk through the doorways easily?
❏	❏	Is there space to maneuver while opening and closing doors?
❏	❏	Does the front door have a view panel or peephole at the correct height?

Appliances, Kitchen, and Bath

Yes	No	
❑	❑	Is the room arranged safely and conveniently?
❑	❑	Do the oven and refrigerator open easily?
❑	❑	Are stove controls clearly marked and easy to use?
❑	❑	Is the counter the correct height and depth?
❑	❑	Can you work sitting down?
❑	❑	Are cabinet doorknobs easy to use?
❑	❑	Are faucets easy to use?
❑	❑	Do you have a handheld shower head?
❑	❑	Are the items you use often on high shelves?
❑	❑	Do you have a step stool with handles?
❑	❑	Can you easily get into and out of the tub or shower?
❑	❑	Do you have a bath or shower seat?
❑	❑	Are there grab bars where needed?
❑	❑	Is the water heater regulated to prevent scalding or burning?

Lighting and Ventilation

Yes	No	
❑	❑	Are there enough lights, and are they bright enough?
❑	❑	Do you have night lights where needed?
❑	❑	Is area well ventilated?

Electrical Outlets, Switches, and Alarms

Yes	No	
❑	❑	Can you turn switches on and off easily?
❑	❑	Are outlets properly grounded to prevent a shock?
❑	❑	Are extension cords in good shape?
❑	❑	Do you have smoke detectors in all key areas?
❑	❑	Do you have an alarm system?
❑	❑	Do you use a personal emergency response system?
❑	❑	Is the telephone readily available for emergencies?
❑	❑	Does the telephone have volume control?
❑	❑	Can you hear the doorbell ring throughout the entire house?

Emergency Preparedness

Preparation Steps

- ❑ Check insurance policies for wind, flooding, fire, or other storm damage coverage
- ❑ Determine evacuation plan
    - ❑ Plan for special assistance if mobility is an issue
    - ❑ Register with local fire department
    - ❑ Have an escape chair if in a high-rise building
    - ❑ Register with utility company if using electrical medical equipment
    - ❑ Have backup supply of oxygen
    - ❑ Store cold packs for medication that needs refrigeration
    - ❑ Prepare food for special dietary needs
    - ❑ Pack food for service dogs
    - ❑ Maintain a supply of water
- ❑ Prepare emergency kit
    - ❑ Adult diapers
    - ❑ Cash and coins
    - ❑ Cell phone chargers
    - ❑ Contact lens solution
    - ❑ Credit/debit/ATM cards
    - ❑ Directions to shelter or evacuation route
    - ❑ Extra pair of glasses
    - ❑ Extra prescription drugs
    - ❑ Flashlight and extra batteries
    - ❑ First aid kit and manual
    - ❑ Hearing aid batteries
    - ❑ Map of area
    - ❑ Matches in waterproof container
    - ❑ Moist towelettes
    - ❑ Personal medication record

- ❑ Portable battery-powered TV or radio
- ❑ Toilet paper
- ❑ Copies of important papers in waterproof/fireproof box
  - ❑ Birth certificate
  - ❑ Blank checks
  - ❑ Passport
  - ❑ Driver's license
  - ❑ Health insurance cards
  - ❑ Insurance policies
  - ❑ List of bank accounts
  - ❑ List of credit/debit/ATM card numbers
  - ❑ List of type and model numbers of medical equipment
  - ❑ Marriage certificate
  - ❑ Medical records
  - ❑ Medicare card
  - ❑ Personal property inventory
  - ❑ Social Security card
  - ❑ Printout of the checklists in this book
- ❑ Telephone tree of emergency contacts
  - ❑ Designate an out-of-state person to be a point of contact
- ❑ Plan for care of pets

Taking Care of Myself

All the time	Never	Needs work	
			I eat healthfully
			I sleep enough
			I get adequate exercise
			I take breaks
			I pursue my hobbies
			I have a network of friends and family I can rely on
			I have people I can talk to
			I take time to have fun
			I ask for help when I need to
			I take steps to manage stress and difficult emotions
			I'm gentle with myself when things go wrong
			I recognize what I can't or don't have time to do
			My finances are in order
			I get annual physicals
			I visit the dentist twice a year
			My employer knows about my caregiving responsibilities

CHAPTER 2

OUR CAREGIVING TEAM

Caregiving takes teamwork. The quarterback of the team is the person you're caring for. Then there's the coach; maybe that's you. You also may have—or need—others on the team. The person you're caring for always, to the greatest extent possible, needs to be kept in the huddle, calling the plays and making the decisions. As with any winning team, the players work together to support the quarterback and execute the game plan as the quarterback directs. The coach on the sidelines looks at the big picture and decides which teammates need to go into the game for the next play. We've all seen a coach put different players into the game depending on what the next play needs to be.

Like football coaches with the clipboard of team players and game plans, caregiving coaches need to see the overall picture and have readily accessible lists of the many team players they can call on. You need to know whom to call for support, answers, and services for many different issues.

Use the checklists in this chapter to organize your team and keep track of who is doing what and when. You'll have all the contact information you'll need if, say, a care provider doesn't show up, medication needs to be picked up, the faucet springs a leak, or the grass needs cutting. With these checklists, you can more easily schedule appointments with doctors and schedule friends and family to drop by or bring dinner. You can quickly contact the lawyer to review contracts, draft documents, help you apply for benefits, and advise you on any legal issues that develop. You'll be able to immediately access the financial professionals to help you manage investments, prepare taxes, and find assets to pay for care and other expenses.

Your employer and the Department of Veterans Affairs (VA) are two possible sources of help to execute the game plan. When you are working and caregiving, you need your employer to be on your team. If the person you are caring for is a military veteran, support is available. The checklists in this chapter help you identify the benefits or support you have or need.

If you don't have, or if you can't find, enough team support, I urge you to look at the resources in this book. Caregiving is tough enough; you do not have to do it alone.

My To-Do Checklist

Done	Need to Do	
❏	❏	Keep track of who on the caregiving team is doing what
❏	❏	Know whom to call in an emergency
❏	❏	List all who provide personal services
❏	❏	List health professionals
❏	❏	List financial professionals and know the different types available
❏	❏	List legal professionals and know how to find them
❏	❏	Check out help from your employer
❏	❏	Take advantage of support available to veterans and their caregivers

✓ Keep track of who on the caregiving team is doing what

To manage the many things that need to be done while caring for another, it's good to divide the tasks into small jobs and spread them among others on the team. Whether they're considered tasks, chores, or jobs, these responsibilities have to be carried out by someone. One person can't do everything; the tasks can be too overwhelming, and no one has every skill and all the time that's needed. Sometimes it's hard to delegate responsibility, but doing so can save caregivers' sanity. Nevertheless, the more people who are involved in care, the greater the need to know who is doing what and when you can expect that task to be completed. Use the Team Tasks Checklist to help you and the rest of the team keep track of who is responsible for what. If the task needs to be done routinely (for example, once a month or ongoing), note that on the checklist. If the job has to be done by a certain time, make sure that person knows the deadline.

✓ Know whom to call in an emergency

Every caregiver knows that things happen. Complications develop when you least expect them: People don't show up, appointments are canceled, plans don't work out, toilets back up, your boss needs you to stay late, the aide's car breaks down. You need backup. The Backup Care/Emergency Checklist is the caregiver's life raft. You might, for instance, have the next-door neighbor's telephone number handy so you can ask her to run over and check on your dad when you're running late and he's not answering his phone. If your home health care aide fails to show for a shift, you'll have the agency's number to call for an emergency replacement. List family members and friends you can call to cover for you when you have to go out of town. My sister was the primary caregiver for our mother because I lived hundreds of miles away, but she knew that when she had to travel for work, she could count on me to be there as soon as I could get a flight.

✓ List all who provide personal services

Lots of people and companies can help with care services. Use the Care and Services Contacts Checklist to record meal and grocery delivery services, the hair salon or barbershop, the volunteer friendly visitor program, the home health care agency, and so on. This checklist notes how to reach the veterinarian, lawn service, property manager, house cleaner, accountant, banker, car mechanic, and many others you may need to contact. Be sure to include contacts for the home security and personal emergency response systems.

Despite everyone pitching in to help, you may find it necessary to hire someone to help provide care at home. Start by making a list of what you want the helper to do. Is it companionship and light housekeeping for a few hours a week, a few hours of respite care, or around-the-clock assistance with injections or catheter care? Some care workers do housekeeping, meal preparation, and laundry as well as provide companionship. Others provide more hands-on care, assisting with activities of daily living such as bathing, toileting, and dressing. Those who can assist with medications, surgical dressings, or other skilled nursing tasks need to have special training, licensing, or certifications. Checklists in Chapter 6 outline what should go into the contracts when you hire professionals, whether you do so on your own or through an agency.

✓ List health professionals

Another long contact list is for medical professionals. The Health Contacts Checklist includes primary care and specialty doctors as well as any therapists, physical trainers, pharmacists, dentists, and audiologists.

Next to the names of medical providers, you may want to record the mileage to their offices (which you can look up on Google Maps or mapquest.com) because the cost of driving to and from medical appointments may be deductible as a health care expense. When it comes time to do taxes, all you need to do is multiply the mileage by the number of trips to that office made each year.

✓ List financial professionals and know the different types available

Many different types of financial professionals can assist you in managing investments, developing an investment strategy, or setting up a withdrawal plan from pensions or other retirement accounts. Which type of professional you should consult depends on what investment help you need.

Certified public accountants (CPAs) are licensed by a state to offer a variety of accounting services including tax preparation, financial audits, business valuations, and succession planning for small businesses.

Daily money managers help with budgeting and bill paying, typically on an hourly basis.

Enrolled Internal Revenue Service (IRS) agents are federally licensed tax preparers who are qualified to represent clients before the Internal Revenue Service. They have passed a comprehensive IRS examination or are former IRS employees.

Fee-only advisers are paid a specific fee for each service.

Financial planners generally take a broad view of a client's financial affairs. They may develop a comprehensive plan to meet investment goals or generally advise you on financial matters. They may also manage an investment portfolio.

Insurance agents can help with health, long-term care, and life insurance, among others, as well as annuities.

Investment advisers generally focus on managing investments. Most are paid by taking a percentage of the assets they manage.

Stockbrokers buy and sell stocks and bonds and are paid by commissions on the trades they make. Some brokers also provide financial planning services.

Before hiring any financial professionals, always ask what licenses or certifications they hold, the types of services they offer, the typical clients they work with, and how they will be compensated. Get in writing how and how much you are going to pay for services— whether you are paying a retainer fee up front, being charged a set fee for each service, or having a percentage or commission deducted from any transaction.

You can often get information on financial professionals using online resources:

- Brokerages, brokers, and investment advisers: www.finra.org/brokercheck
- Certified financial planners: www.cfp.net/search
- Certified public accountants: www.aicpa.org/FORTHEPUBLIC/
- Insurance agents: www.naic.org
- Investment advisers: www.adviserinfo.sec.gov

Use the Financial Contacts Checklist when you need to contact the financial advisers the person you care for has been using or to reach those assisting you with caregiving financial matters.

✓ List legal professionals and know how to find them

You may want to have a lawyer on your team for a variety of different needs. You may want someone to advise you about any legal issues that you face as a caregiver. The person you care for may need to draw up legal documents, such as a power of attorney or a will. You may need legal assistance to draft a family care agreement or to review contracts from assisted living and other residential facilities. Use the Legal Contacts Checklist to record lawyers your loved one is using and the steps you took to hire legal counsel.

When thinking about hiring a lawyer for any type of legal service or advice, you have to answer two related questions: What do you want the lawyer to do, and who is most qualified to perform that service for you? Of key importance is finding a lawyer who has experience in that area of the law and in proper jurisdiction. Cousin Tim who went to law school may not be the best choice if Tim does not have experience with elder law matters. The experienced lawyer in Michigan may not be sufficiently familiar with Texas law to answer a Texas Medicaid question. You'll want to find a lawyer who is licensed to practice and concentrates a substantial part of her or his practice in the state where your loved one lives.

A good way to find a lawyer is to ask friends and family who have recently used the lawyer on a similar matter for their recommendations. Another way is to contact the local or state bar association's lawyer referral service. The American Bar Association has a directory of lawyer referral services available in each state at http://apps.americanbar.org /legalservices/lris/directory/home.html. You may also want to consult the list of elder law attorneys who are members of the National Academy of Elder Law Attorneys at www .naela.org or fellows who are members of the American College of Trust and Estate Counsel at http://www.actec.org/public/roster/FindFellow.asp.

You'll want to interview several lawyers to learn of their expertise, talk about what you think you want the lawyer to do for you, and find out how the lawyer will charge for those services. Lawyers charge for their services in a variety of ways. They can charge an hourly rate or a set fee for providing specific services. Some ask for a lump sum retainer before beginning any work. The lawyer would then draw down disbursements from the retained amount at the hourly rate as work is accomplished. It may be that at first the lawyer cannot calculate the total fee until gaining a better understanding of the problems that might develop. You should, however, expect a detailed and frequent statement of services so you can keep tabs on what has been done and what is being charged.

It is essential that you and the lawyer have the same expectations about what services are to be provided. You may want the lawyer to walk you through the steps you need to take to handle the issue on your own but be available to call from time to time for guidance when you run into a question. On the other hand, you may want the lawyer to handle all details so you don't have to worry about getting everything done. You will want to have a signed letter of engagement that sets out in some detail what the lawyer is going to do for you.

Keep in mind that most lawyers concentrate their practices in some specific areas. For example, tax attorneys concentrate their practices on complicated tax matters. They can assist with the preparation of tax returns and give advice on how to avoid unnecessary taxes. Enrolled agents, who must pass a comprehensive exam, are able to represent you before the IRS. CPAs and lawyers can also represent you before the IRS.

✓ Check out help from your employer

Caregiving is work that can take lots of time. If you also have a job in the workplace, your time may be doubly committed. You may need to be at a meeting at the same time your dad needs to go to the doctor. You may need to interview a new housekeeper for your mom, but have a report for your boss that is due. Amy Goyer, in her book about juggling life, work, and caregiving (www.AARP.org/CaregivingBook), expertly details all the complications and conflicts working caregivers experience every day as well as how to make sure your employer is part of your caregiving team. More and more employers are recognizing the importance of accommodating the needs of employees who shoulder caregiving responsibilities with flexible work conditions and leave policies. Use the Employer Leave Policy and Other Caregiver Supports Checklist to be sure you are aware of all your employer's leave policies and support services.

✓ Take advantage of support available to veterans and their caregivers

The VA has a number of services specifically for people who are caring for veterans. In the United States, there are 5.5 million military caregivers, according to research by the Rand Corporation. Of these caregivers, 1.1 million are caring for someone who served in the military after the terrorist attacks of September 11, 2001.

Every VA medical center has a Caregiver Support Program coordinated by a caregiver support coordinator who serves as a resource expert for veterans and their families. The National Resource Directory (www.nationalresourcedirectory.gov) is an excellent tool to find specific information about services and resources for veterans and those who care for them at the national, state, and local levels. The following are some of the more common services that assist military caregivers:

Respite care. Help to give the caregiver a short-term, temporary break. It could be in-home care, a short stay in an institution, or adult day care for the veteran.

Patient advocate or case manager. An individual who is a liaison between the veteran, care providers, and the caregiver to coordinate care.

Helping hand. Direct support such as loans, donations, legal guidance, housing support, and transportation assistance.

Financial stipend. Compensation for a caregiver's time devoted to caregiving activities or for loss of wages due to caregiving commitments.

Social support. Online or in-person caregiver support groups to assist with caregiving-specific stresses or challenges.

Religious support. Spiritual-based guidance or counseling.

Wellness activities. Family leisure and recreational activities, fitness classes, or stress-relief lessons that focus on improving the caregivers' mental or physical well-being.

Education or training. In-person or online classes, webinars, manuals, or workbooks that provide education related to caregiving activities.

Post-9/11 Caregiver Program. A program specially created to assist caregivers of veterans who were seriously injured in the line of duty on or after September 11, 2001. Eligible caregivers can receive these benefits:

- a monthly stipend based on the veterans' personal care needs
- travel expenses, including lodging and per diem, while accompanying veterans who are undergoing care

- access to health care insurance through CHAMPVA
- mental health services and counseling
- comprehensive caregiver training specializing in caring for those with multiple severe traumas
- respite care

Aid and Attendance. Aid and Attendance (A&A) is a way to receive an increased VA pension amount if the veteran meets one of the following conditions:

- The veteran requires the aid of another person to perform personal functions required in everyday living, such as bathing, feeding, dressing, toileting, or adjusting prosthetic devices.
- The veteran is bedridden in that the disability requires that the veteran remains in bed apart from any prescribed course of convalescence or treatment.
- The veteran is a patient in a nursing home due to mental or physical incapacity.
- The veteran's eyesight is limited to a corrected 5/200 visual acuity or less in both eyes, or concentric contraction of the visual field to 5 degrees or less.

Home- and community-based services. Supports and services offered to the veteran either directly by the VA or by local providers who contract with the VA. Services, provided in the community or in the veteran's home, could include skilled home health care, homemaker/home health aide services, community adult day health care, hospice and palliative care, and veteran directed care.

Nursing home care. Nursing-home-level care in VA-owned and operated community living centers, state-owned and operated veterans' homes, and privately owned facilities that contract with the VA to provide care. Each program has separate admission and eligibility criteria, but the VA pays the full cost for eligible veterans.

Patient-Aligned Care Teams. Teams that provide primary care in the home.

Geriatric Evaluation and Management. An inpatient or outpatient short-term comprehensive geriatric evaluation and management.

Refer to Chapter 11 for explanations of additional veterans' burial benefits.

Our Caregiving Team
Action Checklists

The following Action Checklists are included in Chapter 2:

❑   *Team Tasks*

❑   *Backup Care/Emergency Contacts*

❑   *Care and Services Contacts*

❑   *Health Contacts*

❑   *Financial Contacts*

❑   *Legal Contacts*

❑   *Employer Leave Policies and Other Caregiver Supports*

❑   *Veteran's Caregiver Supports*

Team Tasks

❏ The following members of our caregiving team do these tasks.

Task	Who	When to Complete
Ongoing or periodic help		
❏ Shop for groceries	_____	_____
❏ Sort mail	_____	_____
❏ Help with bills	_____	_____
❏ Clean house	_____	_____
❏ Do laundry	_____	_____
❏ Order and pick up medications	_____	_____
❏ Help with bathing, toileting, grooming, dressing	_____	_____
❏ Take to barbershop/hair salon	_____	_____
❏ Prepare/deliver meals	_____	_____
❏ Walk pets	_____	_____
❏ Take pets to vet/groomer	_____	_____
❏ Do minor household repairs	_____	_____
❏ Cut grass/lawn care	_____	_____
❏ Accompany to and take notes at medical appointments	_____	_____
❏ Accompany to worship services	_____	_____
❏ Coordinate caregivers	_____	_____
❏ Check in by phone or email	_____	_____
❏ Visit	_____	_____
One-time help		
❏ Develop list of people to contact	_____	_____
❏ Set up family phone tree or social media network	_____	_____
❏ Organize photos	_____	_____
❏ Check out adult day care facilities	_____	_____
❏ Identify alternative transportation	_____	_____
❏ Sign up for and track direct deposits	_____	_____

❏   Sign up for and track automatic payments   _____   _____

❏   Create list of log-ons and passwords   _____   _____

❏   Inventory safe deposit box   _____   _____

❏   Get copy of credit report   _____   _____

❏   _____   _____   _____

❏   _____   _____   _____

❏   _____   _____   _____

❏   _____   _____   _____

❏   _____   _____   _____

❏   _____   _____   _____

❏   _____   _____   _____

❏   _____   _____   _____

❏   _____   _____   _____

❏   _____   _____   _____

❏   _____   _____   _____

❏   _____   _____   _____

Backup Care/Emergency Contacts

Family: _____

Home phone: _____ Email: _____

Cell phone: _____

Address: _____

_____

Family: _____

Home phone: _____ Email: _____

Cell phone: _____

Address: _____

_____

Friend: _____

Home phone: _____ Email: _____

Cell phone: _____

Address: _____

_____

Friend: _____

Home phone: _____ Email: _____

Cell phone: _____

Address: _____

_____

Neighbor: _____

Home phone: _____ Email: _____

Cell phone: _____

Address: _____

_____

Faith community: _____

Phone: _____ Email: _____

Website: _____

Address: _____

_____

Geriatric care manager: _____

Work phone: _____ Email: _____

Cell phone: _____ Website: _____

Address: _____

_____

Home care agency: _____

Phone: _____ Email: _____

Website: _____

Address: _____

_____

Social services agency: _____

Phone: _____ Email: _____

Website: _____

Address: _____

_____

Building manager: _____

Phone: _____ Email: _____

Website: _____

Address: _____

_____

Care and Services Contacts

Home health care agency: _____

Phone: _____ Email: _____

Website: _____

Address: _____

_____

Meal delivery: _____

Phone: _____ Email: _____

Website: _____

Address: _____

_____

Meal preparation: _____

Phone: _____ Email: _____

Website: _____

Address: _____

_____

Meals on Wheels: _____

Phone: _____ Email: _____

Website: _____

Address: _____

_____

Grocery delivery: _____

Phone: _____ Email: _____

Website: _____

Address: _____

_____

Household chores: _____

Phone: _____ Email: _____

Website: _____

Address: _____

_____

House cleaning: _____

Phone: _____ Email: _____

Website: _____

Address: _____

_____

Home maintenance: _____

Phone: _____ Email: _____

Website: _____

Address: _____

_____

Property manager: _____

Phone: _____ Email: _____

Website: _____

Address: _____

_____

Plumber: _____

Phone: _____ Email: _____

Website: _____

Address: _____

_____

Car maintenance: _____

Phone: _____ Email: _____

Website: _____

Address: _____

_____

Lawn care/Gardener: _____

Phone: _____ Email: _____

Website: _____

Address: _____

_____

Transportation services: _____

Phone: _____ Email: _____

Website: _____

Address: _____

_____

Taxi company: _____

Phone: _____ Email: _____

Website: _____

Address: _____

_____

Paratransit: _____

Phone: _____ Email: _____

Website: _____

Address: _____

_____

Area agency on aging: _____

Phone: _____ Email: _____

Website: _____

Address: _____

_____

Senior center: _____

Phone: _____ Email: _____

Website: _____

Address: _____

_____

Day care center: _____

Phone: _____ Email: _____

Website: _____

Address: _____

_____

Resident facility manager: _____

Phone: _____ Email: _____

Website: _____

Address: _____

_____

Volunteer services: _____

Phone: _____ Email: _____

Website: _____

Address: _____

_____

Daily money manager: _____

Phone: _____ Email: _____

Website: _____

Address: _____

_____

Accountant: _____

Phone: _____ Email: _____

Website: _____

Address: _____

_____

Banker: _____

Phone: _____ Email: _____

Website: _____

Address: _____

_____

Insurance agent: _____

Phone: _____ Email: _____

Website: _____

Address: _____

_____

Tax preparer: _____

Phone: _____ Email: _____

Website: _____

Address: _____

_____

Friendly visitor: _____

Phone: _____ Email: _____

Website: _____

Address: _____

_____

Spiritual leader/Pastor/Priest: _____

Phone: _____ Email: _____

Website: _____

Address: _____

_____

Faith-based pastoral care: _____

Phone: _____ Email: _____

Website: _____

Address: _____

_____

Hair care: _____

Phone: _____ Email: _____

Website: _____

Address: _____

_____

Veterinarian: _____

Phone: _____ Email: _____

Website: _____

Address: _____

_____

Security system maintenance: _____

Phone: _____ Email: _____

Website: _____

Address: _____

_____

Emergency response service (medical alert): _____

Phone: _____ Email: _____

Website: _____

Address: _____

_____

Health Contacts

Acupuncturist: _____

Phone: _____ Email: _____

Website: _____

Address: _____

_____

Round-trip mileage: _____

Audiologist: _____

Phone: _____ Email: _____

Website: _____

Address: _____

_____

Round-trip mileage: _____

Cardiologist: _____

Phone: _____ Email: _____

Website: _____

Address: _____

_____

Round-trip mileage: _____

Dentist: _____

Phone: _____ Email: _____

Website: _____

Address: _____

_____

Round-trip mileage: _____

Massage therapist: _____

Phone: _____ Email: _____

Website: _____

Address: _____

_____

Round-trip mileage: _____

Music therapist: _____

Phone: _____ Email: _____

Website: _____

Address: _____

_____

Round-trip mileage: _____

Neurologist: _____

Phone: _____ Email: _____

Website: _____

Address: _____

_____

Round-trip mileage: _____

Nutritionist: _____

Phone: _____ Email: _____

Website: _____

Address: _____

_____

Round-trip mileage: _____

Optometrist: _____

Phone: _____ Email: _____

Website: _____

Address: _____

_____

Round-trip mileage: _____

Pharmacist: _____

Phone: _____ Email: _____

Mail-order website: _____

Address: _____

_____

Round-trip mileage: _____

Physical therapist: _____

Phone: _____ Email: _____

Website: _____

Address: _____

_____

Round-trip mileage: _____

Physical trainer: _____

Phone: _____ Email: _____

Website: _____

Address: _____

_____

Round-trip mileage: _____

Podiatrist: _____

Phone: _____ Email: _____

Website: _____

Address: _____

_____

Round-trip mileage: _____

Primary care physician: _____

Phone: _____ Email: _____

Website: _____

Address: _____

_____

Round-trip mileage: _____

Specialty physician: _____

Phone: _____ Email: _____

Website: _____

Address: _____

_____

Round-trip mileage: _____

Specialty physician: _____

Phone: _____ Email: _____

Website: _____

Address: _____

_____

Round-trip mileage: _____

Specialty physician: _____

Phone: _____ Email: _____

Website: _____

Address: _____

_____

Round-trip mileage: _____

Specialty physician: _____

Phone: _____ Email: _____

Website: _____

Address: _____

_____

Round-trip mileage: _____

Speech therapist: _____

Phone: _____ Email: _____

Website: _____

Address: _____

_____

Round-trip mileage: _____

Other: _____

Phone: _____ Email: _____

Website: _____

Address: _____

_____

Round-trip mileage: _____

Financial Contacts

❑ The person I care for uses the following financial professionals:

Name: _____

Firm: _____

Phone: _____ Fax: _____

Address: _____

_____

Email: _____ Website: _____

Account #: _____

Name: _____

Firm: _____

Phone: _____ Fax: _____

Address: _____

_____

Email: _____ Website: _____

Account #: _____

Name: _____

Firm: _____

Phone: _____ Fax: _____

Address: _____

_____

Email: _____ Website: _____

Account #: _____

❑   The person I care for needs to engage a financial professional.

Recommendations received:

Name: _____

Firm: _____

Phone: _____ Fax: _____

Address: _____

_____

Email: _____ Website: _____

   ❑   I have verified the credentials and complaint history.

   ❑   I understand how the financial professional will be paid.

   ❑   The person I care for has a letter of engagement.

Name: _____

Firm: _____

Phone: _____ Fax: _____

Address: _____

_____

Email: _____ Website: _____

   ❑   I have verified the credentials and complaint history.

   ❑   I understand how the financial professional will be paid.

   ❑   The person I care for has a letter of engagement.

Name: _____

Firm: _____

Phone: _____ Fax: _____

Address: _____

_____

Email: _____ Website: _____

   ❑   I have verified the credentials and complaint history.

   ❑   I understand how the financial professional will be paid.

   ❑   The person I care for has a letter of engagement.

❏   The person I care for has identified the following services to receive from the financial professionals:

_____

_____

_____

_____

_____

❏   The person I care for wants to ask the following questions of the financial professionals:

_____

_____

_____

_____

_____

Legal Contacts

❑   The person I care for uses the following legal help:

Name: _____

Firm: _____

Phone: _____ Fax: _____

Address: _____

_____

Email: _____ Website: _____

Name: _____

Firm: _____

Phone: _____ Fax: _____

Address: _____

_____

Email: _____ Website: _____

❑   The person I care for needs to engage legal help.

Recommendations received:

Name: _____

Firm: _____

Phone: _____ Fax: _____

Address: _____

_____

Email: _____ Website: _____

❑   I have verified the complaint history with the bar association.

❑   Recommended by _____

❑   I understand how the lawyer will be paid.

❑   The person I care for has a letter of engagement.

Name: _____

Firm: _____

Phone: _____ Fax: _____

Address: _____

_____

Email: _____ Website: _____

❑   I have verified the complaint history with the bar association.

❑   Recommended by _____

❑   I understand how the lawyer will be paid.

❑   The person I care for has a letter of engagement.

❑   The person I care for has identified the following services to receive from the lawyer:

_____

_____

_____

_____

_____

❑   The person I care for wants to ask the following questions of the lawyer:

_____

_____

_____

_____

_____

Employer Leave Policies and Other Caregiver Supports

❏   My employer has work accommodations or leave policies that are related to my caregiving responsibilities.

Name of employer: _____

Contact for human relations department: _____

Address: _____

_____

Phone: _____ Fax: _____

Email: _____ Website: _____

❏   Highlights of accommodation policies:

Work schedule adjustments: _____

_____

_____

Compressed work week: _____

_____

_____

Flextime: _____

_____

_____

Telecommuting: _____

_____

_____

Part-time position: _____

_____

_____

Job sharing: _____

_____

_____

Phased retirement: _____

_____

_____

Caregiving leave: _____

_____

_____

Family and medical leave: _____

_____

_____

Military caregiver leave: _____

_____

_____

Vacation leave: _____

_____

_____

Sick leave: _____

_____

_____

Bereavement leave: _____

_____

_____

Personal leave: _____

_____

_____

❑ Highlights of support services:

Employee assistance program: _____

_____

_____

Caregiver support group: _____

_____

_____

Health and wellness program: _____

_____

_____

Counseling benefit: _____

_____

_____

Legal assistance benefit: _____

_____

_____

Concierge services: _____

_____

_____

Geriatric care management services: _____

_____

_____

Backup care: _____

_____

_____

Other support services: _____

_____

_____

Veteran's Caregiver Supports

❑   The person I care for served in the U.S. military.

Name veteran served under: _____

First	*Middle*	*Last*

Military service number (DD-214): _____

Date entered active service: _____

Date separated from active service: _____

Service post-9/11:   Yes   No

Type of discharge: _____

Branch: _____

Grade or rank: _____

National Guard: _____

Reserves: _____

VA Medical Center: _____

Address: _____

Caregiver support coordinator: _____

Phone: _____

Email: _____

As a veteran's caregiver, I am eligible (or I will investigate eligibility) for the following benefits through the VA, service organizations, or other agencies:

❑   Caregiver training

❑   Case manager

❑   CHAMPVA health insurance

❑   Financial stipend

❑   Fitness classes

❑   Housing support

❑   Legal guidance

❑   Loans

❑   Mental health services

- ❏ Patient advocate
- ❏ Recreational activities
- ❏ Respite care
- ❏ Spiritual counseling
- ❏ Support group
- ❏ Stress-relief sessions
- ❏ Travel expenses
- ❏ _____

CHAPTER 3

KNOW WHERE IT IS

As a caregiver, you'll be accumulating piles of papers, documents, utility bills, bank statements, medical records, applications, insurance policies, contracts, and more. Not only do you have to keep your own life in order, but you also need to take care of many details for someone else. To keep from being overwhelmed, off and online, you should set up a system to manage the paperwork so you can keep your personal stuff separate and put your hands on that one document when you need it. Your time is at a premium, so you don't want to waste any of it searching for that bit of information you need right now.

You may also have to help organize papers and personal items collected over the years or even over a lifetime. The home may need significant decluttering to make space for a live-in housekeeper or nurse. You may have to help with downsizing or moving to an independent or assisted living facility. As you help go through the closets, boxes, and even storage units, inventory what's there and watch out for what to save. You don't want to throw out something only to learn later on that you need it. For guidance, refer to the section below on how long to keep documents.

One place to store the most important items is a safe deposit box. Obviously, not everything can, or should, be stored there. Many items wouldn't even fit, and important papers such as advance directives, powers of attorney, medication records, medical records, and insurance cards don't go there. You want those ready at hand, accessible at any time.

Digital records are becoming even more important than paper files. So much of everyone's lives is now online. You'll need a list of all the accounts and the user IDs, passwords, PINs, and access codes. I'll touch on two big issues with digital records: keeping this information secure and privacy laws. You'll also find in this chapter a place to record rewards programs and available balances so reward points don't expire.

My To-Do Checklist

Done	Need to Do	
❑	❑	Locate important information and note where it is
❑	❑	Shred papers that contain personal information
❑	❑	Know how long to keep records
❑	❑	Know where the safe deposit box is, what's in it, and who has access
❑	❑	Keep track of online assets and keep them secure
❑	❑	Check on rewards programs

✓ Locate important information and note where it is

For each document or item on the Where to Find It Checklist, indicate where it is: in a safe deposit box, a fireproof box, a filing cabinet, an electronic file, the emergency preparedness kit, or this book. There might be information on this checklist that you didn't even know you'd need. If you're not sure where something is located, now might be a good time to locate it. As always in this book, just ignore any box on the checklist that doesn't apply.

✓ Shred papers that contain personal information

As you sort through old papers and documents and as new paperwork comes in, you need to know what to keep and what to save. The section on how long to keep records can help. If there's something you don't need to hang onto, don't just throw it in the trash. Identity thieves lurk in trash cans for anything with personal information they can use to open new accounts. These thieves value canceled checks or bank statements with bank account numbers, anything with a Social Security number or credit card information, utility bills, old credit cards, driver's licenses, and any card with a picture identification. Invest in a paper shredder that's strong enough to handle your load.

✓ Know how long to keep records

You'll want to save some records. Here are some guidelines for how long to do so.

Probably Forever

These documents should be safely stored forever:

- Academic records, if needed for employment applications
- Adoption papers
- Baptismal certificates
- Birth certificates
- Death certificates (may be needed for tax purposes or applying for survivor benefits)

- Employment records (any agreements, disciplinary files, and performance reviews)
- Health care power of attorney
- Marriage certificates
- Medical records
- Military records (DD-214)
- Citizenship papers
- Passports
- Power of attorney for finances
- Retirement and pension records
- Social Security card
- Wills and codicils

It Varies

The storage life of the following documents depends on their purpose:

- **Bank statements**: One year or until after tax return filed
- **Bills**: For high-value items, as long as the person has the item to prove value for insurance purposes; one year for anything tax or warranty related; all other bills should be shredded as soon as they have been paid
- **Credit card statements**: If tax-related, seven years; otherwise, statements should be shredded immediately when paid
- **Home improvement receipts**: Until home is sold
- **Home insurance policy**: As long as the home is owned
- **Investment records/IRA statements/brokerage statements**: For quarterly statements, until compared against the annual statement; for annual statements, seven years after the account has been closed or the security has been sold
- **Leases**: Until the tenant has moved and received the deposit back from the landlord
- **Life insurance policy**: The life of policy plus three years
- **Mortgage statements**: The life of the mortgage plus seven years
- **Paychecks/pay stubs**: One year or until the W-2 is received
- **Sales receipts**: The life of the warranty on major purchases such as appliances and electronics; otherwise, toss after compared against the credit card statement or when you're sure it won't be needed for a return
- **Tax documents** (including annual returns and all accompanying documents such as W-2s and charitable and medical receipts): Seven years
- **Utility bills**: Three months unless needed for tax purposes
- **Vehicle records**: Until boat, car, motorcycle, or RV is sold

✓ Know where the safe deposit box is, what's in it, and who has access

Safe deposit boxes provide an affordable place for storing valuables and documents. Safe deposit boxes can protect stocks, bonds, gold, silver, and other valuables from both burglary and fire damage. Other things to store in a safe deposit box are important papers such as a marriage license, deeds to real estate, car titles, and life insurance policies. Documents that need to be readily available or frequently updated, including advance directives and digital passwords, probably shouldn't be kept in a bank box. Use the Safe Deposit Box Checklist to inventory what's in the box.

To protect the property in a safe deposit box, banks restrict who can get into the box as well as when and how they can do so. Safe deposit boxes come with a key. When box owners want to store items or access items, they must use both their key and a bank key simultaneously. For safety precautions, neither key alone will open the box. For further protection, the owner must also provide a signature and identification each time before being allowed to access the box. If the person you care for has a safe deposit box and wants to give you access, he or she will need to go to the bank with you to have your name added to the rental agreement and the signature card. Without authorization from the owner and your signature, you will not be allowed to enter the box.

A safe deposit box, like a bank account, may be owned individually or with another person. Joint or co-ownership gives someone else the authority to access the box. Although co-owners of a safe deposit box have equal access to the box, access does not mean they both own the contents of the box. Putting a diamond ring into a safe deposit box doesn't change the ring's owner or make a gift of the ring to the co-owner of the box. If you have any questions about the rights of a co-owner to a safe deposit box, check with the bank or your attorney.

✓ Keep track of online assets and keep them secure

Be sure not to overlook the Digital Assets Checklist and the Rewards Programs for Airlines, Hotels, and Rental Cars Checklist in this chapter. In our digital age, just about any service on the Internet requires a username, password, or other personal identifier to gain access. We need a code just to unlock a computer or answer a cell phone. User IDs and their associated passwords are essential to gain access to email, electronic banking, online bill paying, bitcoins, iTunes files, e-books, games, Facebook, LinkedIn, Twitter, blog posts, movies, videos, digital photo storage, and shopping sites, to name just some of the most obvious. Similarly, MyMedicare.gov and MySocialSecurity.gov require usernames and passwords to access benefit information. Many other personal records and files may be found or stored online. Even the forms in this book are online at http://ambar.org/caregivers so you can access, update, and store the checklists on your computer.

You need to be aware that you may not have ready access to digital files you're aware of. Even with a log-on and password, you're not always free to access or control the account. When I tried to check on an online payment of our home utility bill, I couldn't get access because the account was only in my husband's name. Most websites and social media, as well as federal and state privacy and computer fraud laws, make it very difficult for anyone other than the account owner to have access to any digital accounts and records. We all recognize the importance of those privacy protections, but in an emergency, they can be huge barriers to you as a caregiver. Most current laws now criminalize, or at least penalize, unauthorized access of computers and digital accounts. Many digital providers are prohibited from disclosing most account information to anyone without the account holder's consent, and most sites aren't very clear, or are silent, about how to go about giving consent to someone else.

What can you do? You can read the privacy or access policies of the websites to learn what they allow. Each site may have different procedures and steps you or the person you care for needs to take to gain access to use or manage the account. What you'll be able to do with one account may be totally different with another. Currently, only a few states have laws permitting an account owner to authorize giving access to a designated agent, but more states are considering such legislation. If you're in one of those states with laws in place, the person you care for may want to authorize you to have access to online accounts in a durable power of attorney.

A word of caution: Be sure to have a secure list of all online accounts with usernames and passwords, and keep it up to date. We all need to change passwords frequently to keep them secure. As valuable as this information is going to be to you, it is a gold mine for identity thieves! Keep this checklist in a very secure place. For more on this topic, see AARP's *Protecting Yourself Online for Dummies*, at AARP.org/ProtectingYourselfOnline.

✓ Check on rewards programs

There's one more place to look that you may not have thought about: frequent traveler programs. Some rewards programs also allow the owner to transfer miles to another traveler. Those miles might be used to have a child or grandchild come for a visit. Hotel or car rental rewards could be used to travel out of town for medical treatment. Read the fine print on the program's website to find out how to transfer miles to another family member. Use available rewards so they don't expire. If the points aren't going to be needed, some programs let you donate them to a worthy cause. On the Rewards Programs for Airlines, Hotels, and Rental Cars Checklist, note how many rewards are in the account and when they expire.

Know Where It Is Action Checklists

The following Action Checklists are included in Chapter 3:

- ❏ *Where to Find It*
- ❏ *Safe Deposit Boxes*
- ❏ *Storage Units*
- ❏ *Digital Assets*
- ❏ *Rewards Programs for Airlines, Hotels, and Rental Cars*

Where to Find It

Record Type	Location
Personal history	
Academic records	
Adoption papers	
Animal care information	
Annulment decrees or judgments	
Appointment book or calendar	
Baptismal certificates	
Birth certificates	
Citizenship papers	
Driver's license	
Educational transcripts	
Employment records	
Keys to home	
Keys to other real estate	
Keys to post office box	
Keys to safe deposit box	
Keys to vehicles	
Lock combinations	
Military separation papers	
Naturalization papers	
Passport	
Photo albums	
Property settlement agreement	
Qualified domestic relations order	
Security system information	
Social Security card	
Tax returns and records	

Record Type	Location
Family history	
Adoption papers	
Birth certificates	
Family tree	
Marriage certificate	
Newspaper articles and mementos	
Photo albums	
Portraits	
Insurance policies	
Annuities	
Life	
Long-term care	
Medical	
Medicare card	
Medicare Supplemental	
Umbrella	
Vehicle	
Benefits	
401(k) agreements/statements	
403(b) agreements/statements	
Disability agreements	
IRA agreements/statements	
Keogh plan agreements/ statements	
Pension agreements	
Simplified employee pension (SEP) agreements/statements	
Social Security benefit statement	
Social Security card	

Banking and savings	
Checking account statements	
Credit union account statements	
Savings account statements	
Investments	
Brokerage account statements	
Certificates of deposit	
Savings bonds	
Real estate	
Deeds	
Home improvement records	
Leases	
Mortgages	
Reverse mortgage	
Tax records	
Time-share agreements and records	
Other assets and debts	
Business records	
Computers	
Heirlooms and collectibles	
Credit card contracts	
Jewelry appraisals	
Jewelry inventory	
Jewelry of value	
Judgments	
Loans	
Vehicle certificates of title	
Warranties	

Record Type	Location
Estate planning	
Durable power of attorney	
Trust agreement	
Will and codicils	
Final wishes	
Advance directives	
Body bequeathal papers	
Celebration of life prearrangements	
Cemetery deed	
Cremation prearrangement agreement	
Ethical will/legacy documents	
Funeral prearrangement agreement	
Health care power of attorney	
Legacy information	
Living will	
Medical records	
Obituary	
People to contact	
Pet continuing care	
Physician orders for life sustaining treatments	
Uniform organ donor card	

Safe Deposit Boxes

❏   The person I care for has the following safe deposit boxes:

Name of institution: _____

Phone: _____ Fax: _____

Address: _____

_____

Email: _____ Website: _____

Box #: _____

Key location: _____

Box rent: _____

People who have access to the safe deposit box: _____

Items stored in this box:

_____

_____

_____

_____

_____

_____

_____

_____

Name of institution: _____

Phone: _____ Fax: _____

Address: _____

_____

Email: _____ Website: _____

Box #: _____

Key location: _____

Box rent: _____

People who have access to the safe deposit box: _____

Items stored in this box:

_____

_____

_____

_____

_____

_____

_____

Name of institution: _____

Phone: _____ Fax: _____

Address: _____

_____

Email: _____ Website: _____

Box #: _____

Key location: _____

Box rent: _____

People who have access to the safe deposit box: _____

Items stored in this box:

_____

_____

_____

_____

_____

_____

_____

Storage Units

❑ The person I care for has the following public storage units:

Storage company: _____

Address: _____

Unit #: _____

Website: _____

Username: _____ Password/PIN: _____

Monthly rent: _____ Autopay: Yes   No

Location of the key or lock combination: _____

Storage company: _____

Address: _____

Unit #: _____

Website: _____

Username: _____ Password/PIN: _____

Monthly rent: _____ Autopay: Yes   No

Location of the key or lock combination: _____

Storage company: _____

Address: _____

Unit #: _____

Website: _____

Username: _____ Password/PIN: _____

Monthly rent: _____ Autopay: Yes   No

Location of the key or lock combination: _____

Digital Assets

❑   The person I care for has designated _____
to serve as agent to have access to digital assets.

❑   Usernames and passwords:

Facebook profile name: _____

Twitter profile name: _____

MySpace profile name: _____

Instagram profile name: _____

Computer password: _____

Smartphone password: _____

Tablet password: _____

Website: _____

Username: _____ Password: _____

Website: _____

Username: _____ Password: _____

Website: _____

Username: _____ Password: _____

Website: _____

Username: _____ Password: _____

Website: _____

Username: _____ Password: _____

Website: _____

Username: _____ Password: _____

Website: _____

Username: _____ Password: _____

Website: _____

Username: _____ Password: _____

Website: _____

Username: _____ Password: _____

Website: _____

Username: _____ Password: _____

Website: _____

Username: _____ Password: _____

Website: _____

Username: _____ Password: _____

Website: _____

Username: _____ Password: _____

Rewards Programs for Airlines, Hotels, and Rental Cars

❑   The person I care for has the following rewards programs:

Airline: _____

Website: _____

Frequent flyer #: _____

Username: _____ Password/PIN: _____

Date miles expire: _____

Current balance: _____

Airline: _____

Website: _____

Frequent flyer #: _____

Username: _____ Password/PIN: _____

Date miles expire: _____

Current balance: _____

Airline: _____

Website: _____

Frequent flyer #: _____

Username: _____ Password/PIN: _____

Date miles expire: _____

Current balance: _____

Airline: _____

Website: _____

Frequent flyer #: _____

Username: _____ Password/PIN: _____

Date miles expire: _____

Current balance: _____

Hotel: _____

Website: _____

Rewards #: _____

Username: _____ Password/PIN: _____

Date rewards expire: _____

Current balance: _____

Hotel: _____

Website: _____

Rewards #: _____

Username: _____ Password/PIN: _____

Date rewards expire: _____

Current balance: _____

Hotel: _____

Website: _____

Rewards #: _____

Username: _____ Password/PIN: _____

Date rewards expire: _____

Current balance: _____

Rental company: _____

Website: _____

Rewards #: _____

Username: _____ Password/PIN: _____

Date rewards expire: _____

Current balance: _____

Rental company: _____

Website: _____

Rewards #: _____

Username: _____ Password/PIN: _____

Date rewards expire: _____

Current balance: _____

CHAPTER 4
MAKING DECISIONS FOR SOMEONE ELSE

As a caregiver, you probably make many decisions about the person you care for. Even if you are the person's spouse, child, or other relative, however, there will be times when being a caregiver does not give you the authority to make important decisions. As important and responsible as the role of caregiver is, that title may need to be supplemented with other titles that give you legal authority to make decisions. Banks, care facilities, government agencies, and other third parties that you need to work with may expect or require that your authority be based on more than being a concerned and loving caregiver.

The core legal reason for this requirement is everybody's right to make his or her own decisions. Those decisions could be bad, foolish, harmful, or irrational. We've all made decisions that turned out to be pretty stupid or not well thought through. Still, individually and as a society, we cherish our independence, personal autonomy, and right to make our own decisions.

Of course, we often look to others to help us make decisions. We seek advice from our friends, family, faith leaders, professionals, and even the Internet or social media to help us decide what to do. Few of us make decisions totally on our own without any input from others, but our decisions are still our own.

At other times, we do want someone else to make decisions for us. We may want a friend to order our dinner at a restaurant when we are unfamiliar with the menu. We could ask a neighbor to decide if our lawn needs watering while we're away on vacation. Those kinds of decisions don't need any legal authority; verbal permission is sufficient. More important decisions, though, such as accessing money to pay bills or signing a resident agreement at an assisted living facility, require legal authority.

How can that decision-making authority be delegated? For the most part, people can delegate the authority to make decisions for them under two conditions: They put the transfer of authority in writing, and when they do so, they appreciate what they are doing.

The most common way to transfer decision-making authority is through legal documents called powers of attorney. A power of attorney is a flexible, convenient, and effective way to say I want you, my agent, to do these things or make these decisions for me. Agents use the written power of attorney to document the authority given to them to make whatever personal, medical, or financial decisions are assigned to them. With that legal document, you can add the title of "agent" to your role as caregiver, conveying that you have the authority to carry out specific wishes and make decisions for the person you care for. Other titles that can convey this authority to make decisions are trustee, which I discuss below; executor, addressed in Chapter 11; and joint owner, covered in Chapter 9.

If someone doesn't have the ability to pick who has that authority, courts can pick who will. Those titles would be guardian, conservator, or estate administrator. The Social Security Administration can give limited decision authority through the title of representative payee. Similarly, the Department of Veterans Affairs (VA) can give limited decision authority through the title of a VA fiduciary; I also discuss these roles in this chapter.

Of course, you may not want to have all those titles with special responsibilities, and other people may already be filling those roles or be better able to do so. It could be that you become the health care agent and someone else pays the bills as financial agent. There can be very good reasons to spread the responsibilities among different people. Family members often divvy up or share tasks depending on distance, available time, and skills. The close-by child could help with day-to-day decisions, and the child in another state could manage the books. Similarly, the daughter who's a doctor might make medical decisions, and the son who's good at managing money might oversee investments. The person you care for may have selected a bank trust officer to be the institutional trustee, or a court may have appointed a professional guardian of the person.

However the responsibilities are divided, it's important for all involved to understand the specifics of their role, appreciate what they can and can't do, and communicate with any others to work as a team. Everyone with a part in decision making needs to work hand in hand, respecting the others' authority and, to the greatest extent possible, making sure they involve the loved one in any decision.

These responsibilities all involve complex legal issues. When necessary, consult a lawyer who can walk you through any decisions that need to be made and draw up the necessary paperwork.

My To-Do Checklist

Done	Need to Do	
❑	❑	Know what it means to be an agent with a power of attorney
❑	❑	Know what it means to be a trustee
❑	❑	Know what it means to be a representative payee or VA fiduciary
❑	❑	Know what it means to be a guardian

✓ Know what it means to be an agent with a power of attorney

To complement your role as a caregiver, you may at some point need additional legal authority to make decisions on behalf of the person you care for. Authority to make financial decisions can be given by creating a power of attorney that gives to another person, called the agent or attorney-in-fact, the authority to make decisions when they become unable to do so. (I cover health care powers of attorney in Chapter 5.)

As useful as a power of attorney can be, there are frequently many misunderstandings about the basics of this arrangement:

- You can't get a power of attorney over someone; it has to be given to you.
- The person creating the power of attorney (called the principal) must have the legal capacity to understand the authority being delegated.
- Agents have authority to do only those things that are given to them.
- Agents must make decisions the way the person giving the authority wants, not the way they would do for themselves.
- A lawyer should help draft the power of attorney.

Powers of attorney can be very flexible and can be designed to fit any anticipated needs. The person giving the powers, called the principal, can determine what responsibilities and duties the agent will have. The principal may want to give the agent general powers to do everything that the principal could do, or just specific powers. A power of attorney could grant the authority, for instance, to manage investments, pay bills, collect debts, file lawsuits, sell real estate, negotiate with insurance companies, sell a home or a car, access bank accounts, sign income tax returns, apply for public benefits, or make gifts to charities.

Powers of attorney can differ depending on when the principal wants the agent to be able to act. A *durable* power of attorney begins when signed and stays in effect for the principal's lifetime—even after becoming incapacitated—unless it is canceled. In most states, principals must put specific words in the document stating that the agent's powers stay in effect even after they become incapacitated. The wording to make powers durable is along the lines of "I intend for my agent to continue to have the authority to act on my behalf even if I become incapacitated." In those states that have adopted the Uniform Power of Attorney Act, the law presumes that the principal wants the agent to act after incapacity and the durable wording is not necessary. Check with a lawyer about state law.

The principal can also delay the time when the agent is to begin to act. This option is called a *springing* power of attorney because the effectiveness of the document springs into effect at some time after the document is signed. It could be on a specific date in the future or when a certain event happens. The lawyer must carefully draft a springing power of attorney to avoid any difficulty in determining exactly when the springing event has happened.

Creating a power of attorney does not mean the principal has lost the right to manage his or her own affairs. The principal does not give up anything; instead, he or she is getting an understudy waiting in the wings to help out when needed. Think of a power of attorney as an extra set of car keys that someone else holds. The car's owner has one set and controls when and how that extra set of keys can be used. The owner can take back the keys, give the keys to someone else, and still do the driving. When the owner can't or doesn't want to drive, someone else has the keys to do the driving.

Too many times, lawyers hear from family members that they want to "get a power of attorney over Mom" because they are unhappy with Mom's choices and think they can make better decisions. That's neither the purpose of a power of attorney nor the way it works. The role of an agent is to act on behalf of the principal, carrying out the wishes and directions of the principal. The agent doesn't take over and make decisions for the principal; rather, the agent makes sure the principal's decisions are accomplished.

If the person you care for has selected you to be the agent, you have big responsibilities ahead. Making decisions on behalf of someone else and managing someone else's financial affairs is far more difficult than making your own decisions. Depending on the responsibilities assigned, your job description could include serving as a good financial manager and being totally trustworthy, organized, diligent, and experienced with dealing with bankers, insurance agents, government officials, real estate agents, financial advisers, and tax preparers.

You must understand the limits and scope of your authority. For example, you can only do those things mentioned in the power of attorney. If authority to sell a home isn't given, you can't do it. After the principal dies, your authority ends. You must stop paying the bills and notify the banks and businesses you've been dealing with of the death.

As an agent, you are a fiduciary with fiduciary duties. That means you must do the following:

- Respect the principal's wishes and act only in his or her best interests.
- Involve the principal in the decision making as much as possible.
- Realize that any money you are managing is not your own. It's not your money!
- Manage all assets carefully, even more carefully than your own.
- Keep good records of everything you spend or receive.
- Separate the principal's funds from yours.

Given all the responsibilities you have as an agent, your job may not be easy. Like Rodney Dangerfield, you may feel like you "don't get no respect" in that some businesses or banks may be reluctant to honor your authority, even if you have a power of attorney in hand.

If the person you care for wants you to have access to bank accounts, be sure you both go to the bank to sign the bank's authorization forms and signature card. Typically, a bank has its own forms to fill out before you will be able to access a particular account. It can be a problem if the person you care for has lost the capacity to consent, so it's best to get things squared away at the bank as soon as possible. If a business refuses to accept the power of attorney, ask to speak to a supervisor. Some state laws require businesses to accept powers of attorney unless there is a good reason to not do so. You'll need to make multiple copies of the power of attorney; never give out the original. It's a good idea to keep track of every place you've given a copy. Whenever you sign any document, you should sign as "(my name), as agent for (person you are caring for)."

Being an agent can cause tension with family members. You can avoid concerns with open lines of communication. Be willing to let others know about how or why you made major decisions or explain how you engaged the principal in making the decision. It may help to share your records or prepare a summary of accounts to demonstrate how you are managing the assets. If the principal authorized you to be paid for your services, be sure to keep accurate records of the time you spend acting as agent. Avoid using cash and never make gifts to yourself unless specifically authorized in the power of attorney. These types of practices raise concerns about how agents are managing another's money and if they have any conflicts of interest. If family members are unhappy with your decisions, you may want to get help with a family mediator or other trusted neutral party.

The Consumer Financial Protection Bureau has a guide, *Managing Someone Else's Money: Help for Agents under a Power of Attorney*, at www.consumerfinance.gov/blog /managing-someone-elses-money/.

✓ Know what it means to be a trustee

Trusts can be set up in many different ways and have many different names and purposes. A living trust is a legal arrangement in which someone transfers property to the trust so it can be managed on behalf of the grantor. It is called a living trust because it is created while the grantor is still alive. A testamentary trust is created after death in a will. Both living and testamentary trusts can be revocable (changed or canceled) or irrevocable (cannot be amended). Depending on how it is set up, a trust can be a way to manage finances and to pay for the cost of care.

Every trust has three parties: the *grantor*, the *trustee*, and the *beneficiary* or beneficiaries. The same individual can be all three at the same time. Many grantors who create a living trust (also called the settlor or trustor) name themselves as the trustee because they want to manage the trust as long as they can. They also name a successor trustee who takes over the trust management when they are no longer willing or able to be the trustee and then after the grantor's death. Grantors can also name themselves as the principal trust beneficiary so they can receive the trust proceeds to support them while they are alive. They could also name residuary beneficiaries with instructions on when and how the trust assets are to be held and distributed after their death. In this way, a trust serves a very similar purpose to a will because it directs how any trust assets are distributed to the named beneficiaries.

In addition to creating the trust document, the grantor must also "fund" the trust by preparing deeds, retitling assets, reassigning brokerage accounts, and taking other steps to transfer ownership of the property the grantor wants in the trust. Because the grantor must transfer legal ownership to the trust, the property in the trust no longer legally belongs to the grantor and therefore is not part of the probate assets.

Here's an example of how a living trust works for a trustee. Say your mother set up and funded a trust, naming herself the primary beneficiary of the trust. She served as trustee for several years but now is unwilling or unable to keep up those responsibilities. She named you as successor trustee, and it is time for you to take over. You now have the responsibility to follow the instructions in the trust on how to manage the trust property to take care of her needs. You only have responsibility for the assets in the trust, and you only have the authority stated in the document.

As a trustee, you are a fiduciary. That means you must manage and spend the trust assets only on her behalf and in her best interest. If she named other beneficiaries, either co-beneficiaries during her life or residuary beneficiaries after her death, you have a fiduciary duty to respect their interests, too. You'll need to carefully identify the assets in the trust, make sure they are safe and secure, and keep them separate from your own money and any of her assets not in the trust. Change locks and get insurance for property, if necessary. Make sure bank accounts earn interest and have low fees. You'll need to carefully invest the assets, getting advice from a financial professional about safe and legal investments to have in the portfolio. If the trust permits you to make gifts, you should talk with a lawyer about the Medicaid and tax implications and your mother's plans to distribute trust assets to other beneficiaries after her death. Keep detailed records of all transactions and carefully review all bank, brokerage, or other financial statements.

After her death, you will continue to follow the instructions in the trust to distribute remaining assets to the residuary beneficiaries. In many ways, your responsibility is very much like that of the executor of her will. Both the trust and the will have distinct instructions about what to do with specific property. The trustee, however, is only responsible for managing and distributing the trust property. How much is trust property depends on what assets the grantor decided to put into the trust. In general, the executor, who gets instructions through the will, is responsible for everything that isn't trust property or assets that have a designated beneficiary.

✓ Know what it means to be a representative payee or VA fiduciary

If the person you care for receives Social Security benefits but is unable to manage those funds, you will need to apply for specific authority to receive and manage the benefits. Being a caregiver, agent with a power of attorney, guardian, joint owner on the bank account, or even a spouse does not give you any authority to spend those benefits. Other federal benefit programs, such as veterans' or railroad retirement, and some state government benefits also have similar requirements for a representative to be designated to manage payments on behalf of a beneficiary.

You need to apply to Social Security to be designated the representative payee, or for short, rep payee. Before beginning the application process, it's a good idea to call Social Security at 800-772-1213, read *A Guide for Representative Payees* and check out the frequently asked questions at www.socialsecurity.gov/payee. You will need to submit an application form (SSA 11) along with a doctor's report stating that the person you care for is unable to manage Social Security benefits and have a face-to-face interview with a Social Security representative at a local Social Security office.

Once you are appointed, the benefit payments come to you. You'll need to set up a separate bank account where the benefit will be directly deposited. The bank account must be in the beneficiary's name and show that you are the representative payee. You can use the money only for the needs of the beneficiary, such as rent, food, and clothing. Any money left over after paying expenses should be saved in an interest-bearing savings account or savings bonds for future expenses. Rep payees do not have authority over any other money, property, or medical decisions. That's why it is important to have a bank account just for the Social Security payments that you use to pay only the beneficiary's bills.

As a rep payee with the responsibility to manage someone else's money, you are a fiduciary. All fiduciaries must follow specific standards. You must act in the best interests of the beneficiary, use the money to meet the beneficiary's needs, keep the funds separate from your own or any other money, and report how you have used the money. You cannot lend the money to anyone else or sign leases or contracts, and you cannot pay yourself for managing the funds. Have bills sent directly to you, pay the bills on time, and review the bank statements carefully.

You must keep accurate records of the money you receive and spend and each year file an accounting to the Social Security Administration. Its *Guide for Representative Payees* has a worksheet you can use to keep track of the money. The reporting form is at www .socialsecurity.gov/payee/form/index.htm. You also need to inform Social Security about any changes in address or circumstances that would affect eligibility for the benefit.

The VA has a similar process to select VA fiduciaries, with the same requirements on how to manage the veteran's benefits. Check out *A Guide for VA Fiduciaries* at www .benefits.va.gov/FIDUCIARY/Fid_Guide.pdf.

The Consumer Financial Protection Bureau has a guide, *Managing Someone Else's Money: Help for Representative Payees and VA Fiduciaries*, at www.consumerfinance.gov /blog/managing-someone-elses-money/.

✓ Know what it means to be a guardian

Guardianship should only be considered as a last resort, but if the person you care for becomes unable to make decisions and doesn't have in place the legal tools (powers of attorney; representative payeeship, discussed below; and living trusts, discussed earlier) to grant decision-making powers on his behalf, obtaining guardianship may be necessary for his protection and safety. If the person you care for doesn't have the capacity to make his own decisions, you would ask a court to appoint you as guardian.

What is "capacity"? There's no cut-and-dry answer. It's a term that people use all the time, but with many different meanings. As Amy Goyer explains in her book about juggling life, work and caregiving (www.AARP.org/CaregivingBook):

> A person might have the capacity to do some things but not others. For example, she may have lost the ability to drive, but she may be capable of writing a will or deciding where to live. Further complicating the issue is

that a person's capacity to do any one thing can fluctuate over time and even day to day.

Various formal and informal assessments can be done to evaluate capacity. A driving examiner may determine that your father no longer has the capacity to drive. A lawyer may determine that your aunt doesn't have sufficient capacity to sign a contract but does have capacity to write a will. A doctor might determine that your mother doesn't have the capacity to make a medical decision; after some treatment, however, her capacity to make the next medical decision may return.

In most circumstances, the so-called guardianship alternatives, such as financial and medical powers of attorney, representative payeeship, VA fiduciary, and perhaps a living trust, are all the legal tools needed to make decisions and manage resources on behalf of those who do not have the ability to do so on their own. But powers of attorney and living trusts need to be set up while the person has the capacity to do so. If there's been no advance planning to put these options in place before the person loses capacity, it's too late to rely on them.

Capacity in the context of guardianship is even more complex. Every state has its own definition of the level of incapacity needed to allow the appointment of a guardian.

Before making the leap to petitioning for guardianship, consider the following questions:

- What can I do to help support the person I care for in making decisions on his own, by including input from his circle of friends, family, or advisers?
- What alternatives to guardianship are available, such as powers of attorney for financial and medical decisions, representative payeeship, VA fiduciary, or a living trust?
- If alternatives are available, why have they not been used or failed to work?
- What are the specific areas of decision making where he has such a deficit that his right to make that decision needs to be taken away by the court?
- What rights or powers should remain with him, such as the right to vote, to drive, to privacy, or to decide where to live?

The procedural details to obtain guardianship vary from state to state, so you'll need to consult with an elder law attorney to find out the process in your state. In general, someone who believes a loved one needs a guardian files a petition with the court setting out the reasons why a guardianship is necessary. A medical, mental, or functional assessment must accompany the petition. The petition must be served on the person (called a respondent or alleged incapacitated person), with notice of the reason for the petition and the date of the hearing. In most states, a lawyer will be appointed to represent the respondent. Most likely, a guardian ad litem, court visitor, or other third party selected by the court will interview the petitioner and the respondent to review the facts of the petition and to report to the court if there is a way to avoid or limit the guardianship. The hearing before the judge may be brief or extensive, depending on the circumstances. The respondent has the right to attend and offer testimony or witnesses. In a few states, a jury may determine if the respondent is incapacitated.

The judge needs to determine three things: (1) whether the respondent's condition meets the state's definition of incapacity, (2) what decision-making powers to remove from the respondent and delegate to the guardian, and (3) who should be appointed as guardian. The judge then issues an order setting out the guardian's powers. The powers granted may be broad, or they may be limited to specific decision areas, such as making medical decisions or placing the person in a nursing home.

If a court has appointed you as a guardian for your loved one, you are legally responsible for following the court's order and state guardianship laws. Depending on the order, you may be a guardian of the person with responsibilities to make decisions for her about personal matters, such as where to live or what medical treatment to receive. If you are appointed as guardian of property (called conservator in some states), you are responsible for managing the individual's assets, paying bills, making investments, and filing taxes. As a guardian over financial matters, you are a fiduciary, with fiduciary duties. That means you must act only on behalf of the individual under guardianship, manage the money wisely, keep your money separate, and keep good records so you can report to the court how you have been managing the money. Ask your lawyer if you have any questions about what you can or cannot do.

Although the court order tells you what you can do, most guardians get little guidance about how to make those decisions. A good place to start is the National Guardianship Association's *Standards of Practice* (www.guardianship.org). These standards have been developed by experienced guardians from around the United States. You'll find step-by-step guidance on what you need to consider as you go about making a decision on behalf of someone else. The standards explain, for example, how to ethically consent to medical treatment, change a residence, or decide whether to sell property.

Keep in mind that the decisions you need to make for someone else may not be the decisions you'd make for yourself. You may have to ignore your own interests and resist pressure from others because it is your duty to do what is best for your loved one. You should also involve her in the decisions as much as possible. She may have difficulty making important decisions—you wouldn't have been appointed guardian if that weren't the case—but with your help and encouragement, she should participate in as many decisions as possible.

Managing someone else's money is never easy. Always keep in mind one cardinal rule for guardians of property: It's not your money! Other points flow from this rule:

- Identify all income and property that belong to your loved one and that you are responsible for managing.
- Protect all property. Doing so may mean changing locks, obtaining a safe-deposit box or a secure storage unit, moving money to bank accounts with lower fees, or getting insurance.

- Report all these assets (and any debts) to the court by the due date.

- Create separate guardianship accounts for the funds you are managing. The account should show that it is your loved one's money and that you are the guardian with authority to make deposits and withdrawals.

- Don't borrow, lend, or give away any money that you are managing on behalf of your loved one.

- Make gifts only if approved by the court and if the gift is like gifts your loved one gave in the past.

- Avoid any conflicts of interest, such as paying family members to do work for your loved one.

- Create a budget so you'll know how much you'll need to spend to pay for your loved one's needs for food, clothing, shelter, medical care, medications, and insurance.

- Keep detailed records, statements, and receipts for everything you receive and spend as a guardian.

- Report to the court all income and expenses. Most courts require guardians to file an accounting at least annually.

- Pay yourself for time spent serving as guardian only if the court permits you to do so and only after the court has approved the amount. Keep detailed records of what you did, when you did it, how much time it took, and why you did it.

The Consumer Financial Protection Bureau has a guide, *Managing Someone Else's Money: Help for Court-Appointed Guardians of Property and Conservators*, at www.consumerfinance .gov/blog/managing-someone-elses-money/.

Making Decisions
for Someone Else
Action Checklists

The following Action Checklists are included in Chapter 4:

❏ *Agent with a Power of Attorney*

❏ *Trustee*

❏ *Representative Payee/VA Fiduciary*

❏ *Guardian*

Agent with a Power of Attorney

- ❑   The person I care for has a power of attorney for financial management.
- ❑   The following person is the financial agent:

Agent's name: _____

Phone: _____ Email: _____

Address: _____

- ❑   The person I care for has named me to be the agent to manage his or her financial affairs.
- ❑   I have a copy of the power of attorney.
- ❑   The power of attorney is durable: Yes   No
- ❑   The person I care for has discussed his or her expectations with me, and I understand what my loved one wants me to do as agent.
- ❑   The power of attorney gives me the responsibility to make the following decisions:

_____

_____

_____

_____

_____

_____

- ❑   The co-agents: _____
- ❑   I have talked with the co-agent(s) about how we will work together.
- ❑   My responsibilities begin _____.
- ❑   My responsibilities will last until _____.
- ❑   I can receive the following compensation for serving as agent: _____
- ❑   I have completed all necessary paperwork with financial institutions to have the powers given to me recognized.
- ❑   I have set up a recording keeping system to keep track of all transactions I make that includes what I've done, when I did it, how much time I spent, and why I did it.

❑   The following lawyer is advising me on power of attorney matters:

Name: _____

Phone: _____ Email: _____

Website: _____

Address: _____

_____

❑   The following agencies, financial institutions, or other entities have been given
     copies of the durable power of attorney:

Name: _____

Phone: _____ Email: _____

Address: _____

_____

Name: _____

Phone: _____ Email: _____

Address: _____

_____

Name: _____

Phone: _____ Email: _____

Address: _____

_____

Name: _____

Phone: _____ Email: _____

Address: _____

_____

Name: _____

Phone: _____ Email: _____

Address: _____

_____

© American Bar Association

Trustee

❑ I am trustee or successor trustee under a trust.

❑ I have a copy of the trust.

❑ I have discussed the purpose of the trust with the person I care for and understand what she wants me to do as trustee.

❑ The trust gives me the responsibility to make the following decisions:

_____

_____

_____

_____

_____

_____

❑ The co-trustees of the trust: _____

❑ I have talked with the co-trustee(s) about how we will work together.

❑ My responsibilities begin _____.

❑ My responsibilities will last until _____.

❑ I can receive the following compensation for serving as trustee: _____

❑ The co-beneficiaries of the trust: _____

❑ The residuary beneficiaries of the trust: _____

❑ I have inventoried all assets and property included in the trust (see Chapters 8 and 9).

❑ The assets in the trust include the following: _____

_____

_____

_____

_____

_____

❑ I have created a trust bank account (see Bank Accounts Checklist in Chapter 7).

❑ I have created a budget to include any expenses to be paid out of the trust (see Expenses Checklist in Chapter 7).

❏ I have set up electronic deposit of income and automatic payment of bills through the trust.

❏ I have secured and insured all property that I'm responsible for through the trust (see the insurance checklists in Chapter 10).

❏ I have set up a recording keeping system to keep track of all transactions I make that includes what I've done, when I did it, how much time I spent, and why I did it.

❏ The lawyer advising me on trust matters:

Name:_____

Phone: _____ Email:_____

Website:_____

Address:_____

_____

❏ The financial professional advising me on trust investment matters:

Name:_____

Phone: _____ Email:_____

Website:_____

Address:_____

_____

❏ I have notified the following agencies, financial institutions, or individuals that I am the trustee:

_____

_____

_____

_____

_____

_____

Representative Payee/VA Fiduciary

❑ The Social Security Administration has selected me as the representative payee.

❑ The Veterans Administration has selected me as the VA fiduciary.

❑ The benefit amount: _____

❑ I have created a fiduciary bank account for benefit payments.

❑ I have set up electronic deposit of the benefit.

❑ I have created a budget to pay for food, housing, clothing, and medical needs.

❑ I have set up a recording keeping system to keep track of all expenses paid.

❑ Date my first accounting report is due: _____

Guardian

❏   The court has appointed me guardian of person.

❏   The court has appointed me guardian of property.

❏   The court has given me the responsibility to make the following decisions:

_____

_____

_____

_____

_____

_____

❏   The guardianship order was granted on _____.

❏   I have obtained bonding as ordered by the court in the amount of _____.

❏   My personal status report is due to the court on _____.

❏   I have done an inventory of all assets, property, and debts that I'm responsible for (see Chapters 7, 8, and 9).

❏   My inventory is due to the court on _____.

❏   My first accounting is due to the court on _____.

❏   I have created a guardianship bank account (see Bank Accounts Checklist in Chapter 7).

❏   I have set up electronic deposit of income and automatic payment of bills.

❏   I have secured and insured all property that I'm responsible for (see the insurance checklists in Chapter 10).

❏   I have applied to be the representative payee or VA fiduciary for any Social Security or veterans' benefits (see Social Security Benefits Checklist in Chapter 7).

❏   I have set up a recording keeping system to keep track of all decisions I make, including what I've done, when I did it, how much time I spent, and why I did it.

❏   I have created a plan of care.

❏   I have created a budget to cover expenses (see Income Checklist and Expenses Checklist in Chapter 7).

❏   I have applied for any eligible benefits (see Public Benefits Checklist in Chapter 7).

❏   I have a current photograph of the person I care for.

❑ I have notified the following agencies or individuals of my appointment (see the contacts checklists in Chapter 2):

_____

_____

_____

_____

_____

_____

CHAPTER 5
MEDICAL MATTERS

Medical issues loom large among caregivers' responsibilities. You probably spend a lot of time making sure the person you care for stays healthy or gets well. Time is often spent arranging healthy meals, scheduling and going to medical appointments, picking up medications, and waiting in hospitals, for example.

As a caregiver, you will need to have a fairly extensive knowledge of the medical history of the person you care for, including recent surgeries and hospitalizations. It's also important to be aware of all current medications and have a handy list of prescriptions, over-the-counter drugs, and vitamins as well as drug allergies and interactions. The checklists in this chapter help you manage your time and organize the medical information you need.

In this chapter, I also cover making decisions for someone else regarding health care. (Chapter 4 addresses other types of decisions.) Just about everyone wants and has the legal right to make his or her own health care decisions. At the same time, many people want to get help and advice from those around them before making more difficult or complex medical decisions. Others want or need to authorize someone else to make the decisions for them. If the person you care for has signed an advance directive giving you the ability to make decisions and give medical consent, be sure to understand what you can and cannot do and how you are supposed to carry out your responsibilities. This chapter will walk you through all that and explain terms you may need to understand, such as DNR (do not resuscitate) and POLST (physician orders for life-sustaining treatment).

My To-Do Checklist

Done	Need to Do	
❑	❑	Compile a medical history
❑	❑	Compile and carry a personal medication record
❑	❑	Understand your role as a health care agent
❑	❑	Understand any DNR or POLST in place

✓ Compile a medical history

Use the Medical History Checklist in this chapter to note a comprehensive medical history and to track drug allergies, surgeries, or hospitalizations. Having this information at your fingertips will better equip you to help handle current and future medical needs. You can add the doctor treating the condition, when the condition was cured, or any other pertinent information about that condition.

✓ Compile and carry a personal medication record

On the Personal Medication Record Checklist in this chapter, list all prescription drugs as well as any over-the-counter drugs, vitamins, or herbal or dietary supplements taken by the person you are caring for. Also include the reason for each medication as well as the pharmacy and prescribing physician, if any. If you are not sure why a medication is prescribed, ask the prescribing doctor. You can also list the form of the medication, such as a pill, liquid, patch, or injection, and dosage, such as how many milligrams in each tablet. Note the frequency of the medication, too, such as "one pill at breakfast," and any special directions, such as "with food."

You, the person you care for, and team members who help with medical appointments should carry a copy of the Personal Medication Record all the time and share this information with all doctors and pharmacists. At each appointment, review the list with the doctors. Email fulfillment@aarp.org for additional personal medication records worksheets in a vinyl sleeve to carry with you. Ask for C2470 (English) or C2387 (Spanish). They are free.

✓ Understand your role as a health care agent

An advance directive is a legally accepted way to tell health care providers the types of care a person would want if he were unable to communicate his preferences and who he wants to make decisions about that care when he cannot do so. An advance directive has two parts: a *living will* and a *health care power of attorney* (HCPOA).

A living will outlines the treatments the patient would or would not want if he were unable to communicate and his death was imminent, or if he were permanently unconscious, in a vegetative state, or at the end stage of a chronic condition such as Alzheimer's disease.

In most states, the law restricts the circumstances under which a living will is effective. Typically, this document is used to record the patient's wishes concerning specific life-prolonging treatments. It is crucial that family members and doctors understand those preferences concerning treatments, such as the use of respirators, cardiopulmonary resuscitation, or intravenous nutrition or hydration.

The second part of an advance directive is the selection of a health care agent, or proxy, who can speak for the patient only when the patient is unable to do so. This selection is done by signing a *health care power of attorney*. In a health care power of attorney, patients can, if they want, give the agent broad authority to make any health care decision they specify, not about just a life-prolonging treatment. They set down any guidance or instructions they want the agent and health care team to follow. Perhaps more important, they have someone who will speak for them and get necessary information from health care providers to make the decisions they would want to be made on their behalf. Having preferences in writing and someone to speak up on the patient's behalf helps family members make difficult decisions and makes sure the patient's personal values are respected.

If the person you care for hasn't prepared an advance directive, you may want to start this conversation by helping him talk with doctors, spiritual advisers, or others who can help him think through serious medical issues and what brings him quality of life. The Five Wishes advance directive form (www.agingwithdignity.org/five-wishes.php) may be useful in starting and structuring important conversations about the medical care he wishes to have. The American Bar Association also has a kit (http://apps.americanbar.org /aging/publications/docs/consumer_tool_kit_bk.pdf) that is very useful in discussing spiritual values, personal priorities, and more with doctors and family.

After the conversation, the next step is to prepare the advance directive. You don't need a lawyer to draft this document. You can find free state-specific forms at www.aarp.org /advancedirectives and links to other information about advance directives at www .americanbar.org/groups/law_aging/resources/health_care_decision_making.html. Many elder law attorneys will prepare advance directives as part of estate and advance care planning. Most hospitals, area agencies on aging, bar associations, and medical societies also provide free forms.

If you've been asked to serve as the health care agent, it is vitally important that you know and understand the individual's wishes about medical treatments. You will need to feel comfortable talking about end-of-life care and be willing to follow those wishes, even if they are not the same as your own. You need a thorough understanding of what is important to that person for her quality of life and the kind of medical care she does or does not want to have.

As a health care agent, you'll need to be able to talk with health care providers about changing medical conditions and authorize treatment or have it withdrawn as circumstances change. You may need to be assertive when talking with health care professionals. In the sometimes bewildering medical system, you should be a strong advocate who can stand up for what you know the patient would want and take any other necessary steps to see that those wishes are honored, including changing doctors or hospitals if necessary.

You should have copies of the advance directive readily available and make sure health care providers also have copies. The person you care for should carry a wallet card that indicates she has an advance directive and how to get in touch with the health care agent.

✓ Understand any DNR or POLST in place

In addition to health care powers of attorney, you'll also need to know about *do not resuscitate orders* (DNRs), *out-of-hospital DNRs* (OOH DNRs), and the physician orders for life-sustaining treatment form, known as a *POLST*.

Unlike the HCPOA that a patient fills out, a DNR is an order made by a doctor that is placed in the patient's medical record. The DNR directs the hospital medical team to not attempt to revive the patient in the event the patient stops breathing or the heart stops beating. The order will be entered only in those special circumstances where the doctor has confirmed with the patient, when possible, or the health care agent that not trying to restore breathing or heart rhythm is the preferred alternative.

Some states also have provisions for an OOH DNR. This order directs emergency medical service (EMS) responders not to try to revive a patient who is not in a hospital. Under most circumstances and state laws, EMS teams responding to a 911 call are required to make all attempts to revive an unresponsive person. Even if the person has a living will that specifies otherwise, EMS responders cannot honor it. People living at home or in an assisted living facility may not want to be resuscitated, but because of their medical condition, they cannot stop the EMS team from going ahead with cardiopulmonary resuscitation, defibrillation, or other life-sustaining treatments. To overcome this situation, the patient requests an OOH DNR and the doctor enters the order. The patient then wears a special DNR medical alert bracelet. In those states with OOH DNR laws, EMS personnel are trained to look for a DNR bracelet and to know that they can legally not try to revive the person.

All but six states also have POLST protocols. Typically, a state-prescribed POLST form is prepared for very sick patients with multiple chronic conditions. A POLST complements, rather than replaces, an advance directive. Although the details as well as the name (MOST or POST, for example) vary from state to state, this form is used to prompt conversations among medical providers, patients, and families about the patient's current treatment preferences. It records in detail the decisions made by the patient and puts those decisions into medical orders to be followed in a medical crisis. The form is printed on brightly colored paper so that it can be readily seen, followed, and transferred with the patient from hospital to nursing facility and back to the hospital. EMS personnel must honor a POLST. To find out about POLST protocols in the state where the person you care for lives, go to www.polst.org.

Medical Matters
Action Checklists

The following Action Checklists are included in Chapter 5:

❑ *Medical History*

❑ *Personal Medication Record*

❑ *Health Care Power of Attorney*

❑ *Medical Orders (Do Not Resuscitate/POLST)*

Medical History

Yes	Notes
❑ Alcoholism	_____
❑ Allergies	_____
❑ Alzheimer's disease	_____
❑ Arthritis	_____
❑ Asthma	_____
❑ Birth defects	_____
❑ Blood disorder	_____
❑ Cancer	_____
❑ Cataracts	_____
❑ Chromosomal disorder	_____
❑ Chronic obstructive pulmonary disease	_____
❑ Cystic fibrosis	_____
❑ Dementia	_____
❑ Depression	_____
❑ Diabetes	_____
❑ Eczema	_____
❑ Endometriosis	_____
❑ Epilepsy	_____
❑ Gallbladder problems	_____
❑ Gastrointestinal disorder	_____
❑ Glaucoma	_____
❑ Gout	_____
❑ Hay fever	_____
❑ Hearing loss	_____
❑ Heart disease	_____
❑ High blood pressure	_____

Yes   **Notes**

❑ High cholesterol   _____

❑ Inflammatory bowel disease   _____

❑ Infertility   _____

❑ Intellectual disability   _____

❑ Kidney disease   _____

❑ Learning disabilities   _____

❑ Lung disease   _____

❑ Lymphoma   _____

❑ Macular degeneration   _____

❑ Mental disorder   _____

❑ Miscarriage, stillbirth   _____

❑ Muscular dystrophy   _____

❑ Neurological disorders   _____

❑ Obesity   _____

❑ Osteoporosis   _____

❑ Psoriasis   _____

❑ Sickle cell disease   _____

❑ Skin cancer: basal cell   _____

❑ Skin cancer: melanoma   _____

❑ Skin cancer: squamous cell   _____

❑ Stomach disorders   _____

❑ Stroke   _____

❑ Thyroid disorder   _____

❑ Ulcers   _____

❑ Vision impairment   _____

❑ Other   _____

Blood type: _____

Drug allergy/reaction: _____

Drug allergy/reactions: _____

Drug allergy/reactions: _____

Drug allergy/reactions: _____

Surgery: _____

Purpose: _____

Date: _____

Hospital: _____

Doctor: _____

Surgery: _____

Purpose: _____

Date: _____

Hospital: _____

Doctor: _____

Surgery: _____

Purpose: _____

Date: _____

Hospital: _____

Doctor: _____

Hospitalizations: _____

Cause: _____

Date: _____

Hospital: _____

Doctor: _____

Hospitalizations: _____

Cause: _____

Date: _____

Hospital: _____

Doctor: _____

Hospitalizations: _____

Cause: _____

Date: _____

Hospital: _____

Doctor: _____

Hospitalizations: _____

Cause: _____

Date: _____

Hospital: _____

Doctor: _____

Personal Medication Record

Personal Information

Name: _____

Date of birth: _____

Phone number: _____

Emergency Contact

Name: _____

Relationship: _____

Phone number: _____

Primary Care Physician

Name: _____

Phone number: _____

Website: _____

Pharmacy/Drugstore

Name: _____

Pharmacist: _____

Phone number: _____

Website: _____

Pharmacy/Drugstore

Name: _____

Pharmacist: _____

Phone number: _____

Website: _____

Medical Conditions

_____

_____

_____

_____

_____

_____

_____

Allergies

_____

_____

_____

_____

_____

_____

Notes

_____

_____

_____

_____

_____

Medications

Name of medication	Reason	Form	Dosage	When/How	Prescribing physician	Pharmacy

Be sure to include *all* prescription drugs, over-the-counter drugs, vitamins, and herbal or dietary supplements.

Health Care Power of Attorney

❑   The person I care for has a health care power of attorney.

❑   The following person (if not me) is the health care agent:

Agent's name: _____

Phone: _____ Email: _____

Address: _____

_____

❑   The person I care for has named me to be the health care agent.

❑   I have a copy of the health care power of attorney.

❑   The person I care for has discussed expectations with me, and I understand what he or she wants me to do as a health care agent.

❑   The health care power of attorney gives me the responsibility to make the following decisions:

_____

_____

_____

_____

_____

_____

The following health care providers have been given copies of the health care power of attorney:

Hospital: _____

Phone: _____ Email: _____

Address: _____

_____

Hospital: _____

Phone: _____ Email: _____

Address: _____

_____

Doctor: _____

Phone: _____ Email: _____

Address: _____

_____

Doctor: _____

Phone: _____ Email: _____

Address: _____

_____

Doctor: _____

Phone: _____ Email: _____

Address: _____

_____

Doctor: _____

Phone: _____ Email: _____

Address: _____

_____

Assisted living facility: _____

Phone: _____ Email: _____

Address: _____

_____

Nursing facility: _____

Phone: _____ Email: _____

Address: _____

_____

Health care agency: _____

Phone: _____ Email: _____

Address: _____

_____

Medical Orders (Do Not Resuscitate/POLST)

❑ The person I care for does not have a do not resuscitate order (DNR).

❑ The person I care for has a do not resuscitate order (DNR).

❑ The person I care for has an out-of-hospital do not resuscitate order (OOH DNR).

❑ The person I care for wears a state-prescribed out-of-hospital do not resuscitate (OOH DNR) medical alert bracelet.

❑ The person I care for has a physician order for life-sustaining treatment (POLST) form.

Physician who entered the DNR: _____

Phone: _____ Email: _____

Cell phone: _____

Physician who entered the OOH DNR: _____

Phone: _____ Email: _____

Cell phone:_____

Physician who entered the POLST: _____

Phone: _____ Email: _____

Cell phone: _____

The following health care facilities or providers have the medical orders:

Hospital: _____

Phone: _____ Email: _____

Cell phone: _____

Hospital: _____

Phone: _____ Email: _____

Cell phone:_____

Nursing facility: _____

Phone: _____ Email: _____

Cell phone: _____

Assisted living facility: _____

Phone: _____ Email: _____

Cell phone: _____

Health care agency: _____

Phone: _____ Email: _____

Cell phone: _____

Other: _____

Phone: _____ Email: _____

Cell phone: _____

CHAPTER 6
DECIPHERING CONTRACTS

This chapter is all about some of the contracts you may encounter as you go about the business of caregiving. There may be a contract to pay a family member to provide care and contracts to hire outside help such as an attendant or housekeeper. There may be form contracts provided by a home health care agency or residential facility. The person you care for may want to purchase, or have already purchased, a long-term care insurance policy or a pre-need agreement that pays funeral costs in advance. Knowing what to watch out for in these contracts is important to the people you care for and their family members to avoid surprises down the line.

The checklists in this chapter walk you through what should be included in each of these contracts as well as who needs to sign the contracts and how to sign them. You'll find help in understanding the fine print and what to look for and in knowing the important options or terms.

The information in this chapter is just a start. Always have a lawyer review any contract before signing.

My To-Do Checklist

Done   **Need to Do**

❑   ❑   Know what to include in a family caregiver agreement

❑   ❑   Consider whether to hire home care services directly or through an agency

❑   ❑   Be prepared to negotiate the contract if hiring home care services directly

❑   ❑   Make sure you understand the services included in a home care agency contract

❑   ❑   Understand what is and isn't provided in an assisted living facility contract

❏   ❏   Understand what is and isn't provided in a skilled nursing facility contract

❏   ❏   Learn to read the fine print in a long-term care insurance policy

❏   ❏   Know what has been paid for in pre-need funeral arrangements

✓ Know what to include in a family caregiver agreement

A family caregiver agreement can be an appropriate way to pay a family caregiver for the time spent taking care of a loved one. This is especially important if the caregiver has to stop working or reduce hours worked to free up time to be a caregiver. Often, caring for a loved one can be a long-term commitment and a full-time job. For some families, if there are funds available, it's important to compensate family members for the significant amount of time, effort, and money they spend providing care to a loved one. Many families would prefer to keep the money in the family rather than pay a home health care agency for aides or attendants to perform similar services. Paying a family member for caregiving services might help someone who needs care but cannot qualify for Medicaid until the estate is reduced. Some long-term care insurance policies also allow for compensation to family caregivers, but only if there is a formal, reasonable contract.

To be effective, the agreement must be in writing, be signed, set out the specific services the caregiver will provide going forward, and provide "reasonable" compensation. It's also crucial that other family members be involved in the discussions of whether and how to compensate a family member. Having the agreement in writing can clear up other family members' possible resentment or concern that the caregiver is taking advantage of the loved one or getting a larger share of the estate. Medicaid rules also require that any agreement to pay a family member be in writing, at a reasonable fair market value rate, and for actual services provided. Otherwise, Medicaid will consider the payment as a gift, delaying when the person will qualify for Medicaid benefits.

How much to pay is up to the care recipient and family members to decide. It's a good idea to find out how much a home health care agency would charge to provide similar services. The U.S. Administration on Aging has an elder care locator that can lead you to local agencies at www.eldercare.gov. Genworth Financial tracks actual costs for care services across the country at www.genworth.com/corporate/about-genworth/industry-expertise /cost-of-care.html. The family caregiver may be willing to receive less than the average, but the amount paid should be similar to what the family would have to pay a third party. The agreement has to be for future services; it can't cover services already given.

The Family Caregiver Agreement Checklist in this chapter identifies some of the terms that should be considered in creating an agreement:

- What services are to be given in as much detail as possible
- When, how, and how much the caregiver will be paid

- What expenses will be reimbursed
- When services and payment for care are to begin
- When the agreement will be reviewed

Keep in mind that the circumstances of either the care recipient or caregiver may change, making the agreement unworkable. You may want to review the agreement every six months to make sure everyone is happy with the arrangements. Any changes need to be in writing.

Beware of potential tax consequences. The Internal Revenue Service (IRS) is most likely going to consider a family caregiver who is directly employed by the care recipient an "employee" rather an "independent contractor." The IRS uses a number of factors to distinguish between employees and independent contractors, such as whether the person who hires them sets hours and responsibilities, determines the particulars of the job, and directs the activities of the care provider. In contrast, the worker who is hired by a third party, such as an employment agency or private duty service provider, and referred to the care recipient is typically an independent contractor. The family will need to consult with a tax attorney if there are any questions about whether a caregiver is an employee or an independent contractor.

The tax withholding and reporting requirements are simple for independent contractors. The care recipient doesn't need to withhold, report, or pay taxes on wages paid to an independent contractor; those are the responsibilities of the employing agency. As an employer, however, the care recipient must withhold Social Security (known as FICA, after the Federal Insurance Compensation Act); withhold unemployment, state, and federal income taxes; file a W-2; provide a Form 1099; apply for an employer ID; report wages on Schedule H; pay unemployment taxes (known as FUTA, after the Federal Unemployment Tax Act); and pay at least minimum wage. The care recipient may be able to deduct some of the caregiving expenses as medical expenses. The caregiving employee, on the other hand, must pay federal and state income taxes, Social Security and Medicaid taxes; applicable state and local taxes; and possibly a business tax. There are some exclusions for "domestic workers in the private home" of the employer, so check with a tax adviser for the details.

You don't have to have a lawyer draft the agreement, but if you are using the contract for estate or Medicaid planning purposes, you should consult with one. Contact your local bar association's lawyer referral service or the National Academy of Elder Law Attorneys (www.naela.org) to locate a lawyer knowledgeable about Medicaid rules in the care recipient's state. You may also want to involve an outside professional to avoid family friction over how a parent's assets are being used. Having everything set out clearly and accurately as a true employer-employee relationship can minimize complications with Medicaid eligibility and reduce misunderstandings or disagreements among family members about who has responsibility to provide care and how it is to be compensated.

✓ Consider whether to hire home care services directly or through an agency

At some point as a caregiver, you may find it necessary to hire someone to help provide care at home. You have two principal options for finding in-home care services: hire an independent professional directly or go through an agency. Some areas also maintain registries or referral services of independent aides, nurses, and therapists.

Hiring someone directly, rather than through an agency, may be a bit more affordable, but the burden is on the family for screening skills, checking credentials and references, withholding Social Security and taxes, scheduling, arranging a backup plan if the individual can't show up, and supervising the services. Home care agencies can take care of some of the screening, matching, and paperwork, but they are likely to charge a higher hourly rate (and pay the worker less) to cover the supervisory and administrative work they do.

✓ Be prepared to negotiate the contract if hiring home care services directly

If you are hiring directly, use the Independent Home Care Contracts Checklist in this chapter to make sure the necessary terms are negotiated and included in a written agreement. Be specific about the services the individual will provide, work schedule, pay, and benefits covered. Be sure to check references, do a background check, and verify that the individual has the appropriate licensing. Have a lawyer look the agreement over to make sure it is complete.

✓ Make sure you understand the services included in a home care agency contract

The home care agency typically will assess the client's abilities and then match needs to one or more of the workers it has available. The agency should work closely with the client to find someone in its pool of workers who is compatible and has the right skills and training. The agency should also have workers on call who can substitute in case the regular worker can't make it.

All these details and more should be set out in the contract. The agency will most likely have a standard contract that sets out the services the agency provides. Look for clear explanations of how the worker is supervised and how to request a different worker. The contract should include the services to be provided, the specific individual at the agency in charge of supervising care, the worker's schedule, pay rates, and the process for handling grievances and terminating the agreement. Be sure to ask questions about any terms you don't understand. Again, have a lawyer review the contract with you.

You should do some homework before selecting a home health care agency. You'll want to make sure it has the proper licensing to deliver the level of care needed; some agencies may not be able to provide skilled nursing care. If Medicare is going to be providing any help with the cost of care, the agency must be approved by Medicare and the care must be prescribed by an attending physician. To find Medicare-approved home health care agencies nearby, use Medicare's HomeHealthCompare tool at www.medicare.gov /homehealthcompare. You can also check with the local area agency on aging (AAA) for list of home care providers. Go to www.eldercare.gov to find the local AAA. AARP's Caregiving Resource Center also maps local home care agencies and provides user reviews at www.aarp.org/caregiving. Use Medicare's checklist as you check out each home care agency at www.medicare.gov/what-medicare-covers/home-health-care/Home %20Health%20Agency%20Checklist.pdf.

✓ Understand what is and isn't provided in an assisted living facility contract

Whether the person you care for lives in or is considering an assisted living facility, you'll want to understand all the provisions in the contract, even the fine print. Have a lawyer review the contract before it is signed.

If you're considering a few facilities, it's a good idea to read and compare the contract terms. Because not all assisted living facilities are the same, not all admissions contracts are the same. You may have to ask specifically for the contract because it is usually not part of the shiny marketing packet. (You'll also want to check with the long-term care ombudsman, at www.eldercare.gov, in your locality about any documented issues or complaints.)

Ask questions and get an explanation from the facility for any terms in the contract the family doesn't understand. Then be sure to ask the lawyer those same questions, just to verify the facility's explanation. Be wary of facilities that say the contract is standard, it's what everyone signs, or it can't be changed.

Know before the search begins the types or level of services that are needed now and will be needed in the foreseeable future. The person you care for won't want to move in only to find that the facility can't provide what is needed or have to start the search process all over again for a different facility when needs change.

Make sure the types of services or level of care your loved one needs and will receive are spelled out as part of the contract. State regulations may determine the levels of medical care the facility can provide. Just because something is mentioned in the promotional brochure does not mean it will show up in the contract. Compare what is advertised or promised to what is actually mentioned in the contract.

The contract should also explain what medical services are available, such as doctors or nurses on site or on call, assistance with medication, or a preferred pharmacy. Are residents able to use their choice of health care providers, care aides, and pharmacies?

You'll want to know if the person you care for will have a private bedroom or share with others. What is the maximum number of roommates, and what is the procedure if the roommates are not compatible? Residents should have the opportunity to request a room or roommate change. They will want to have personal items within the living space. Be sure you know what personal items the residents can bring with them and what the facility will furnish, such as lounge chairs, special mattresses, sleep sofas or futons for overnight guests, a television, a night stand, or even family pictures. Family members will want to know if they can stay overnight, share meals with the resident, visit at any time, or take the resident out for trips.

Be sure there is clarity about costs. Most assisted living facilities have tiers of services, with higher costs as more services are needed. Care services may have a separate price tag from the costs of room and board. Others may charge for specific services in addition to basic care. Compare the rate schedule for extras such as transportation to medical appointments or events, hair care, guest meals, parking space, exercise room, laundry, and medication delivery. You may also want a list of services the facility is not going to provide.

Other important contract provisions include how long the contract lasts and how to get out of the contract if the choice is not a good fit. Under what conditions can residents get out of the contract, and what refunds or adjustment of any prepaid fees will be made? Is it a month-to-month contract, or is it renewed annually? Will the price increase with each renewal? How frequently will the schedule of fees change, and how much notice is given about a change in rates? Under what circumstances can residents be asked to leave? It could be a change in health status, a lengthy hospital stay, disruptive or unsafe behavior, or failure to pay the monthly charges. Note what the contract says about how the decision is made to change the level of care and what happens if the level of care needed is more than the facility is licensed to provide. Good contracts will also explain residents' rights and the process for filing complaints or grievances.

Who signs the resident agreement contract has significant legal and financial consequences. Ordinarily, the resident would sign, agreeing to the terms of the contract and to be the person responsible for payment of the fees. There may be circumstances when someone else is going to be the "responsible party." If that is you as a caregiver, be sure you appreciate that as the "responsible party" you are personally liable for all payments. If you are an agent with powers of attorney or a guardian, you must make clear to the facility that you are signing on behalf of the resident. You would sign as "(your name), as agent for (resident)." In that way, you would not be personally responsible for the costs.

Before signing any contract, have it reviewed by a lawyer experienced with residential facility issues.

✓   Understand what is and isn't provided in a skilled nursing facility contract

The need for skilled nursing care may arise suddenly, with little time available for comparison shopping. In some areas, available beds are limited and choices may be limited. However emotional the decision to move to a skilled care facility may be, take the time to carefully review the contract before signing it and have a lawyer go over it with you. Admissions contracts are complex, so ask the nursing home about any language that's confusing.

The prospective resident is the only person who should sign the nursing home contract, unless the resident has a guardian or has given authority to an agent with powers of attorney. Guardians, agents, or any others who have legal access to the resident's money and who sign on behalf of the resident will not be personally liable for the costs of care. Family members should only sign the contract as the "responsible party" or "guarantor" if they understand they are liable for the nursing home expenses. Nursing homes cannot require family members to guarantee payment.

Look at what is included in the facility's basic daily or monthly rate. It will usually cover room and meals, housekeeping, linens, general nursing care, medical records services, recreation, personal care, and similar services that are provided equally to all residents. Extra charges in most nursing homes include these services:

- Physician's services, including the work of specialists like dentists, ophthalmologists, and podiatrists

- Medications
- Physical therapy
- Diagnostic services, such as laboratory work, X-rays, and electrocardiograms
- Personal services, such as telephone calls, personal laundry, and hair care

Medicare and Medicaid may cover some of these extra charges. Private-pay residents may be billed for personal services once for the length of the resident's stay, as a flat charge each month, or each time a service or material is provided.

Some of the other contract provisions that the prospective resident needs to watch for include restrictions on applying for Medicaid; limits on visiting hours; and requirements for a family member to guarantee payment, to make a deposit if Medicaid eligible, to have an advance directive or do not resuscitate order on file, to consent in advance to all medical care, or to agree to arbitrate any contract disputes. Also, make sure you understand the "bed hold" policy, which explains what happens if the resident has an extended hospital stay and wants to return to the nursing facility. These contract provisions, and more, are governed by federal and state laws. Use the Skilled Nursing Facilities Contracts Checklist to note provisions that should be reviewed with a lawyer.

✓ Learn to read the fine print in a long-term care insurance policy

Long-term care insurance pays for part of the cost of care. If the person you care for has been paying for this type of policy, you are going to want to understand what the policy does and does not cover to best take advantage of the benefits.

Pre-conditions: Typically, the insurance company will require the policyholder to need assistance with a specific number of activities of daily living and a functional assessment by a doctor the insurance company provides.

Setting: No policy covers all costs of care in any setting. Early policies just covered some of the costs of skilled care in a nursing home. Now, most policies will also pay part of the cost of care at home or in an assisted living facility.

Waiting period: You'll need to read the fine print on the policy to know when benefits kick in. Depending on the policy, there may be a waiting period of zero, 30, 60, or 100 days between the time the person you care for becomes eligible for benefits and the payments start. A longer waiting period reduces the premiums, but also requires the ability to pay out of pocket for the cost of care while waiting.

Payments: The policy will define how much it will pay per day (on average between $150 and $250), any benefit maximum, or other payment terms depending on the type of care.

Deductible: Some policies have a deductible, an amount the policyholder must pay toward the care before the policy pays.

Joint policies: Another option is to have a joint policy that would provide coverage for a couple with a maximum benefit amount to be shared by the couple if both need care.

Medicaid coordination: Some states allow policies to be written to coordinate with the Medicaid program. Policyholders can receive maximum benefits from a partnership-qualified plan and still qualify for Medicaid. The details of the Long-Term Care Partnership Program vary among those states with the program, so check with a local insurance agent or elder law attorney for details. There's a chart of states with partnership programs at www.aaltci.org/long-term-care-insurance/learning-center/long-term-care-insurance-partnership-plans.php.

Because of the multiple policy options, you may want to sit down with an insurance agent and a lawyer to go over the policy so you can understand all its provisions.

✓ Know what has been paid for in pre-need funeral arrangements

Many funeral establishments encourage people to pay a fixed price now for a future funeral. Pre-paying fixes the costs at today's prices for your choice of a coffin and other services that may cost more in the future. Equally important, making financial arrangements in advance can provide peace of mind that arrangements are in place.

The person you care for may want to consider planning for her funeral and ask your assistance in making the arrangements. You can work together to explore the options, understand the costs, and be confident that her wishes will be honored. Before pre-paying for a funeral, get confirmation in writing from the funeral director about how the financial investment will be protected. You want to be assured that the money is in safe hands and the pre-need contract will be honored as much as a decade in the future. With most pre-need contracts, you turn over a sum of money, either a lump sum or in installment payments. The money is then placed in trust held by a third-party trustee or used to purchase an insurance policy. The trustee or insurance company is responsible for managing the money until it is time to pay the funeral home for the goods and services listed in the contract. Ask whether the funds will be securely placed in a trust held by a financially sound third party or used to purchase an insurance policy.

You will also want to ask about the portability of the contract if the person you care for should move to another location and no longer want the funeral where originally planned. If plans change or the funeral home changes hands, you'll want to be able to transfer the contract to a different funeral home.

Before paying for a pre-need contract, check with your state's attorney general or board of funeral directors to learn how pre-need contracts are regulated in your state. Be sure to include the details of the pre-arrangement on the Funeral Pre-Need Arrangements Checklist in this chapter.

There are other options to set aside money to pay for a funeral. Funerals are expensive, on average $7,000 to $10,000. Your loved one may wish to purchase a life insurance policy that would cover the anticipated funeral costs or invest money in a certificate of deposit, pay on death (POD) bank account, or savings account designated to cover these expenses. With such options, you know that the money will be available to cover expenses, but your loved one remains in control of the money as plans for final arrangements change.

Deciphering Contracts
Action Checklists

The following Action Checklists are included in Chapter 6:

❑ *Family Caregiver Agreements*

❑ *Independent Home Care Contracts*

❑ *Agency Home Care Contracts*

❑ *Assisted Living Facility Contracts*

❑ *Skilled Nursing Facility Contracts*

❑ *Long-Term Care Insurance Policies*

❑ *Funeral Pre-Need Arrangements*

Family Caregiver Agreements

❑   The person I care for has a family caregiver agreement.

❑   Date the family caregiver agreement was signed by the caregiver: _____

❑   Date the family caregiver agreement was signed by the care recipient: _____

❑   The family caregiver agreement was signed by _____

     on behalf of the care recipient as _____

     (guardian, agent with financial powers of attorney) on _____.

❑   Date the terms of the family caregiver agreement were discussed with other family members: _____

❑   Lawyer assisting in the drafting of the family caregiver agreement:

     _____

❑   Start date for the agreement: _____

❑   The agreement will be reviewed if there is significant change in the health of the care recipient or caregiver or the ability of the caregiver to perform the services.

❑   End date for the agreement: _____

❑   The agreement can be terminated under these conditions: _____

     _____

❑   The family caregiver agreement covers the following services:

     ❑   Monitor nutritional needs

     ❑   Prepare nutritious, appropriate meals and snacks

     ❑   Shop for groceries

     ❑   Clean house

     ❑   Do laundry

     ❑   Assist with grooming

     ❑   Assist with bathing

     ❑   Assist with dressing

     ❑   Coordinate household bills

     ❑   Shop for clothing, toiletries, and personal care items

     ❑   Arrange for social services, social engagement, and activities

     ❑   Transport to social events

❏ Monitor physical and mental condition

❏ Arrange for medical assessment, services, and treatment

❏ Monitor medication

❏ Schedule medical appointments

❏ Transport to medical appointments

❏ Interact with health care agent, health professionals, long-term care facility administrators, social service personnel, insurance companies, and government workers

❏ Preserve the privacy of the care recipient

❏ Communicate with other family members

❏ Follow the direction of any financial or medical agent

❏ Other: _____

❏ The family caregiver agrees to provide _____ hours of care each week.

❏ The family caregiver's schedule: _____

_____

_____

_____

_____

❏ The family caregiver is considered to be:

❏ An employee

❏ An independent contractor

❏ The care recipient agrees to pay the caregiver as follows:

❏ $ _____ per hour

❏ $ _____ as a lump sum, calculated as follows: _____

_____

❏ The family has discussed the tax and Medicaid implications of a lump sum payment with the following attorney: _____

❏ Median hourly compensation for caregivers in the area: _____ .

❏ The caregiver will be paid _____ weekly _____ biweekly _____ monthly

❑ The caregiver's mileage will be reimbursed at the rate of $ _____ .

❑ The following out-of-pocket expenses will be reimbursed with receipts:

   ❑ Restaurant meals with the care recipient

   ❑ Cell phone

   ❑ Other: _____

❑ Payment for services and reimbursement of expenses will be made on behalf of the care recipient by _____.

❑ The caregiver agrees to keep a daily log of services provided and receipts for all expenses.

❑ The care recipient agrees to withhold the following taxes and file all necessary forms or reports:

   ❑ Social Security (FICA)

   ❑ Federal unemployment

   ❑ Federal income

   ❑ State income

   ❑ State unemployment

   ❑ Worker's compensation

❑ The caregiver understands the responsibility to pay federal and state income taxes and the appropriate share of Social Security and Medicare payments.

❑ The care recipient agrees to provide health insurance for the caregiver as follows:

_____

❑ The care recipient agrees to pay the caregiver for _____ days of respite or paid vacation.

❑ The backup plan for when the caregiver is not available or healthy is as follows:

_____

_____

_____

_____

Independent Home Care Contracts

❑   The person I care for needs to hire an independent home care provider.

❑   The following independent home care providers have been interviewed:

Name: _____

Phone: _____ Email: _____

Address: _____

_____

Reference: _____

Phone: _____ Email: _____

Address: _____

_____

Reference: _____

Phone: _____ Email: _____

Address: _____

Criminal background check: Yes   No

Care license verified: Yes   No

Driver's license verified: Yes   No

Qualifications: _____

Demonstrated skills: _____

Hired: Yes   No

Name: _____

Phone: _____ Email: _____

Address: _____

_____

Reference: _____

Phone: _____ Email: _____

Address: _____

_____

Reference: _____

Phone: _____ Email: _____

Address: _____

_____

Criminal background check: Yes   No

Care license verified: Yes   No

Driver's license verified: Yes   No

Qualifications: _____

Demonstrated skills: _____

Hired: Yes   No

Name: _____

Phone: _____ Email: _____

Address: _____

_____

Reference: _____

Phone: _____ Email: _____

Address: _____

_____

Reference: _____

Phone: _____ Email: _____

Address: _____

_____

Criminal background check: Yes   No

Care license verified: Yes   No

Driver's license verified: Yes   No

Qualifications: _____

Demonstrated skills: _____

Hired: Yes   No

The contract has been reviewed by the following lawyer:

Name: _____

Phone: _____ Email: _____

Address: _____

_____

Contracted services include the following:

- ❏ Personal service
    - ❏ Assist with bathing
    - ❏ Assist with toileting
    - ❏ Assist with grooming, hair care, foot care, shaving
    - ❏ Other: _____
- ❏ Personal care
    - ❏ Carry out the directions of the care plan
    - ❏ Implement exercise routine
    - ❏ Assist with mobility and transfers
    - ❏ Other: _____
- ❏ Medication assistance
    - ❏ Ensure medications taken on time with correct dosage
    - ❏ Manage refill schedule
    - ❏ Note any drug reactions
    - ❏ Other: _____
- ❏ Household services
    - ❏ Laundry
    - ❏ Bed changing
    - ❏ Housekeeping
    - ❏ Other: _____
- ❏ Nutrition
    - ❏ Feeding
    - ❏ Meal preparation
    - ❏ Grocery shopping

❑ Accompany to restaurants

❑ Other: _____

❑ Record keeping

   ❑ Daily log on vital signs

   ❑ Physical condition

   ❑ Behavior changes

   ❑ Patient progress updates

   ❑ Other: _____

❑ Transportation

   ❑ Use client's car

   ❑ Use own car that is insured and registered

      ❑ Policy has liability limits of $ _____ for bodily injury.

      ❑ Policy has liability limits of $ _____ for property damage.

      ❑ Vehicle tag #: _____

   ❑ Transport to medical appointments

   ❑ Transport on errands, shopping, social engagements

   ❑ Other: _____

❑ Medicare care

   ❑ Injections

   ❑ Catheter care

   ❑ Wound dressing

   ❑ IV care

   ❑ Ventilator care

❑ Therapy

   ❑ Physical

   ❑ Speech

   ❑ Occupational

   ❑ Music

   ❑ Recreation

Care provider will report _____ (frequency) to _____ .

Care provider will report emergencies to _____.

Care provider schedule:

- ❏ Days: _____
- ❏ Hours: _____
- ❏ The schedule can be changed if _____
- ❏ Backup plan if care provider is sick or otherwise unable to report on time: _____

  _____

  _____

  _____

  _____

- ❏ Date care services will begin: _____
- ❏ Date probationary period will end: _____

Care provider will be paid:

- ❏ $ _____ per hour
- ❏ Mileage when transporting client at $ _____ per mile

Client will provide:

- ❏ Social Security (FICA) withholding
- ❏ Medicare withholding
- ❏ Federal tax withholding
- ❏ State tax withholding
- ❏ Worker's compensation
- ❏ Paid vacation
- ❏ Health insurance

Household expenses will be paid:

- ❏ Out of household account
- ❏ Approved credit/debit card

❑ Reimbursed with receipts for approved expenditures

❑ Other: _____

The contract can be terminated:

❑ With _____ days' notice

❑ Other: _____

Attorney's fees will be awarded if court action is needed to enforce terms of the contract:
Yes   No

Agency Home Care Contracts

❏ The person I care for needs to hire a home health care provider through an agency.

❏ The following home health care agencies have been interviewed:

Agency name: _____

Contact person: _____

Phone: _____ Email: _____

Address: _____

_____

Referred by: _____

License verified: _____

Checked www.medicare.gov/homehealthcompare: Yes   No

Medicare approved: Yes   No

Accepts Medicaid   Yes   No

Agency name: _____

Contact person: _____

Phone: _____ Email: _____

Address: _____

_____

Referred by: _____

Checked www.medicare.gov/homehealthcompare: Yes   No

Medicare approved: Yes   No

Accepts Medicaid: Yes   No

Agency name: _____

Contact person: _____

Phone: _____ Email: _____

Address: _____

_____

Referred by: _____

Checked www.medicare.gov/homehealthcompare: Yes   No

Medicare approved: Yes   No

Accepts Medicaid: Yes   No

The agency contract has been reviewed by the following lawyer:

Name: _____

Phone: _____ Email: _____

Address: _____

_____

The agency contract was signed by _____.

The person responsible for payment: _____

Services the agency will provide include the following:

- ❑ Personal service
    - ❑ Assist with bathing
    - ❑ Assist with toileting
    - ❑ Assist with grooming
    - ❑ Other: _____

- ❑ Personal care
    - ❑ Carry out the directions of the care plan
    - ❑ Implement exercise regime
    - ❑ Assist with mobility and transfers
    - ❑ Other: _____

- ❑ Medication assistance
    - ❑ Ensure medications taken on time with correct dosage
    - ❑ Manage refill schedule
    - ❑ Note any drug reactions
    - ❑ Other: _____

- ❑ Household services
    - ❑ Laundry
    - ❑ Bed changing
    - ❑ Housekeeping
    - ❑ Other: _____

❑ Nutrition
  ❑ Feeding
  ❑ Meal preparation
  ❑ Grocery shopping
  ❑ Accompany to restaurants
  ❑ Other: _____

❑ Record keeping
  ❑ Daily log on vital signs
  ❑ Physical condition
  ❑ Behavior changes
  ❑ Patient progress updates
  ❑ Other: _____

❑ Transportation
  ❑ Use client's car
  ❑ Use agency or worker's car that is insured and registered
    ❑ Policy has liability limits of $ _____ for bodily injury.
    ❑ Policy has liability limits of $ _____ for property damage.
    ❑ Vehicle tag #: _____
  ❑ Transport to medical appointments
  ❑ Transport on errands, shopping, social engagements
  ❑ Other: _____

❑ Medicare care
  ❑ Injections
  ❑ Catheter care
  ❑ Wound dressing
  ❑ IV care
  ❑ Ventilator care

Date/time agency will conduct functional assessment: _____

Care provider will report emergencies to _____ .

Agency will provide care services as follows:

❑ Days: _____

❑ Hours: _____

❑ The schedule can be changed if _____.

❑ Date care services will begin: _____

❑ Date probationary period will end: _____

Agency fees are as follows:

❑ $ _____ per hour

❑ Mileage when transporting client at $ _____ per mile

Agency will provide:

❑ Social Security (FICA) withholding

❑ Federal tax withholding

❑ State tax withholding

❑ Worker's compensation

❑ Unemployment withholding

❑ Paid vacation

❑ Health insurance

❑ Insurance billing

❑ Medicare billing

❑ Medicaid billing

The contract can be terminated:

❑ With _____ days' notice

❑ Other: _____

Attorney's fees will be awarded if court action is needed to enforce terms of the contract:
Yes   No

Assisted Living Facility Contracts

❏ The person I care for has an assisted living facility contract.

❏ Date the contract was reviewed by a lawyer: _____

❏ Date the contract was signed by the resident: _____

❏ The contract was signed on behalf of the resident by _____

in the legal role of _____.

(agent with power of attorney, guardian)

❏ The term (length) of the contract: _____

❏ Date the contract can be reviewed/renewed: _____

❏ Date the contract can be terminated by resident: _____

❏ The contract can be terminated by facility if _____ .

❏ Intent to terminate requires _____ days' notice.

❏ Levels of care the facility is licensed to provide:

    ❏ _____ with _____ services

    ❏ _____ with _____ services

    ❏ _____ with _____ services

❏ Procedure for change in level of care: _____

❏ Fee schedule for each level of care provided: Yes   No

❏ Price list for extra services provided: Yes   No

❏ Procedure for change in price lists: _____

❏ Initial or application fee of $ _____ is refundable: Yes   No

Procedure for change in ownership or management of the facility: _____

_____

❏ Renter's insurance required: Yes   No

❏ Private room: Yes   No

❏ Maximum number to share a room: _____

❏ Procedure for selecting or changing rooms or roommates: _____

❏ Furnishings provided by facility: _____

❏ Furnishings provided by resident: _____

❏ Responsibility for lost or damaged personal property: _____

❑   Overnight guest policy: _____

❑   Guest meal policy: _____

❑   Visitation restrictions: _____

❑   Grievance procedure: _____

❑   Statement of residents' rights provided: Yes   No

Skilled Nursing Facility Contracts

- ❏ The person I care for has a skilled nursing facility contract.

- ❏ Date the contract was reviewed by a lawyer: _____

- ❏ Date the contract was signed by the resident: _____

- ❏ The contract was signed on behalf of the resident by_____

  in the legal role of_____.

  (agent with power of attorney, guardian)

- ❏ The term (length) of the contract: _____

- ❏ Date the contract can be reviewed/renewed: _____

- ❏ The contract can be terminated by resident under these conditions: _____

  _____

- ❏ Intent to terminate requires _____ days' notice.

- ❏ The contract can be terminated by facility under these conditions:

  - ❏ Necessary for the resident's welfare

  - ❏ Skilled care is no longer required

  - ❏ Health and safety of others is endangered

  - ❏ Failure to pay for services

  - ❏ Facility ceases to operate

- ❏ Levels of care the facility is licensed to provide:

  - ❏ _____ with _____ services

  - ❏ _____ with _____ services

  - ❏ _____ with _____ services

- ❏ Procedure for change in level of care: _____

  _____

- ❏ Facility is Medicare-certified: Yes   No

- ❏ Fee schedule for each level of care provided: Yes   No

- ❏ Basic daily rate includes:

  - ❏ Room

  - ❏ Meals

  - ❏ Housekeeping

  - ❏ Linens

❑   General nursing care

❑   Medical records services

❑   Recreation

❑   Personal care

❑   Other: _____

❑   Price list for extra services not included in the basic rate provided: Yes   No

❑   Procedure for change in price lists: _____

_____

❑   Application fee of $ _____ is refundable: Yes   No

❑   Procedure for change in ownership or management of the facility: _____

_____

_____

❑   Private room: Yes   No

❑   Maximum number to share a room: _____

❑   Procedure for selecting or changing rooms or roommates: _____

_____

❑   Furnishings provided by facility: _____

❑   Furnishings provided by resident: _____

❑   Responsibility for lost or damaged personal property: _____

❑   Overnight guest policy: _____

❑   Guest meal policy: _____

❑   Visitation restrictions: _____

❑   Grievance procedure: _____

❑   Statement of residents' rights provided: Yes   No

❑   Requirement of private pay: Yes   No

❑   Right to apply for Medicare and/or Medicaid: Yes   No

❑   Bed hold policy consistent with Medicare/Medicaid requirements: Yes   No

❑   Limits on liability for residents' injury: Yes   No

❑   Requirement to have advance directive: Yes   No

❑   Requirement to have do not resuscitate order: Yes   No

❑   Requirement to arbitrate disputes: Yes   No

Long-Term Care Insurance Policies

❏ The person I care for has the following long-term care insurance policy:

Policy #: _____

Insurance company: _____

Agent: _____

Phone: _____ Fax: _____

Address: _____

_____

Email: _____ Website: _____

The policy has been reviewed by the following lawyer:

Name: _____

Phone: _____ Email: _____

Address: _____

_____

The policy contains the following terms:

❏ Triggers to begin claiming benefits

    ❏ Inability to perform _____ activities of daily living

    ❏ Evaluation by company's medical professionals

    ❏ Documentation by primary physician

    ❏ Moderate cognitive impairment

    ❏ Required hospital stay of _____ days

    ❏ Other: _____

❏ Waiting period between eligibility and benefit payment of _____ days

❏ Deductible: $ _____

❏ Total days/years of coverage: _____

❏ Benefit maximum: $ _____ Daily rate: $ _____

❏ Joint coverage for _____ and _____

❏ Inflation protection: Yes   No

    ❏ Compound

    ❏ Simple

❏   Premium waiver when benefits begin: Yes   No

❏   Benefit payments are taxable income: Yes   No

Coverage includes:

❏   Home health care expenses

    ❏   Licensed professional required: Yes   No

    ❏   Payment details: _____

❏   Assisted living expenses

    ❏   Certified facility required: Yes   No

    ❏   Payment details: _____

❏   Nursing home expenses

    ❏   Medicare-approved facility required: Yes   No

    ❏   Payment details: _____

❏   Compensation of family caregiver: Yes   No

❏   Adult day care: Yes   No

❏   Care coordination: Yes   No

❏   Reimbursement of home modification: Yes   No

❏   Long-Term Care Partnership Program to qualify for Medicaid: Yes   No

❏   Other coverage: _____

Coverage excludes:

❏   Conditions: _____

❏   Services: _____

Funeral Pre-Need Arrangements

❑ The following pre-need arrangements for a funeral have been made:

Funeral home: _____

Funeral director: _____

Address: _____

Phone: _____

Email: _____

Website: _____

Location of pre-need contract: _____

The pre-need contract guarantees the price of stated goods and services:

❑ Yes

❑ No

The following funeral services have been pre-paid:

❑ Alternative container

❑ Basic professional services

❑ Body preparation

❑ Casket

❑ Copies of death certificate

❑ Crematory fee

❑ Clothing for burial

❑ Embalming

❑ Graveside service

❑ Limousine for family members

❑ Memorial book

❑ Memorial folders or service bulletin

❑ Obituary preparation

❑ Outer burial vault or grave liner

❑ Preparation of photo DVD or CD

- ❏ Public or family viewing or visitation
- ❏ Recording of service
- ❏ Service at the mortuary
- ❏ Transportation of the body
- ❏ Urn for cremains

The person I care for has the following pay on death (POD) account to be used to pay for funeral expenses:

Financial institution: _____

Account #: _____

Name on the account: _____

Amount in the account: $ _____

The person I care for has the following pooled funeral trust or funeral insurance policy:

Account/Policy #: _____

Amount in the trust or policy: $ _____

Insurance company: _____

Contact information: _____

Location of policy: _____

CHAPTER 7
MONEY MATTERS

Caregivers who help manage someone else's money should have a clear financial picture. The checklists in this chapter help you understand what money is (and is not) available and suggest where to look for other sources of assistance to pay for care.

First, you'll want to look at income and money available in bank accounts to pay for expenses, including care services. (Also refer to Chapter 8, where you'll have the opportunity to identify retirement and investment accounts.) If not enough money is coming in, I help you explore whether the person you care for is eligible for Social Security or public benefits and, if so, how to apply. If she or he served in the military, what veterans' benefits could help? Reverse mortgages are a possible source of money to help stay at home, but they are expensive to set up, so it's important to know both the pros and cons.

Part of that financial picture also may include existing debts that reduce the amount of money available to pay for care. You'll want to look at all credit and debit cards. Personal loans may need to be paid back, and any liens or judgments by creditors may need to be taken care of. If the person you care for has gotten behind on payments, you may have to deal with debt collectors. In this chapter, you'll find guidance on what to do and not do if you get those calls.

My To-Do Checklist

Done	Need to Do	
❏	❏	List all income and expenses
❏	❏	Find out what's in the bank
❏	❏	Understand Social Security benefits and how to navigate the system
❏	❏	Check out veterans' benefits
❏	❏	Get a copy of military service records
❏	❏	Apply for other available public benefits
❏	❏	Look for outstanding loans and debts

❏　　　　❏　　　Know how to deal with debt collectors

❏　　　　❏　　　Know how a reverse mortgage works

✓　List all income and expenses

You may need to set up a budget for the people you care for. First, you'll need to help them identify all their income and expenses. What money is available to pay for their care? How much are they paying each month for utilities, rent or mortgage, insurance premiums, out-of-pocket medical expenses, groceries, and more? Use the Expenses Checklist in this chapter to track down how much they need monthly to cover their living expenses. If there's not enough money to pay current expenses and pay for additional care support, you may need to work with them to find ways to cut back. Are there less expensive phone plans? Can they save money on prescription drugs by ordering by mail? If the home were better insulated, could the fuel bill be lower? Are there other benefits they are eligible for? A good source for information about saving money, cutting costs, and budgeting is www.aarp.org/money.

✓　Find out what's in the bank

Once you have the income and bank accounts listed, you'll want to understand the different ways that bank accounts can be titled, or owned. The type of bank account can make a big difference in what money is available to pay for caregiving expenses and what happens to the money on deposit when the account holder dies. Among the possible ways to own bank accounts are these:

- *Individual*: Money in an individual account can be used by the depositor for any purpose and will be distributed according to the terms of a will, or if the depositor does not have a will, according to state law. Only the depositor can access the funds or write checks.

- *Agency or convenience account*: A co-signer can access money in this type of account, but the money in the account does not belong to the co-signer. This is the type of account most people should use if they want a family caregiver to have access to the account to help pay bills. Money remaining in this account will be distributed according to the terms of the will, or if there is no will, according to state law.

- *Joint with right of survivorship*: With a joint account with right of survivorship, all money in the account belongs to both co-owners, and on the death of one of the co-owners the balance automatically goes to the surviving co-owner. Adding a son, daughter, or any other person to an account as joint owner is the same as making a gift of all money now on deposit and any future deposits. The co-owner can write checks for any purpose and could, in fact, withdraw the account down to zero and head for Alaska. For Medicaid purposes, adding a joint owner (other than a spouse) to an account is considered a transfer for less than fair market value and could delay eligibility for Medicaid.

- *Pay on death (POD)*: The person named as beneficiary on this type of account automatically receives the balance in the account on the death of the person who established the account but has no right or authority to access the account until then. The original depositor can change the beneficiary, spend the money, or close the account at any time. Many people set up a POD account to make sure money is quickly available to pay for funeral expenses or final medical bills.

If you need to use money from the bank account to pay bills, you'll need to get legal authority to access those funds. Never sign the name of the person you are caring for on a check or use her ATM card to make withdrawals from an account in her name. There are various strategies you and she can consider. She could ask you to be the agent under a power of attorney to assist with bill paying (see Chapter 4), but even with a signed power of attorney, you're not home clear. The bank will not give you access to any accounts without her express approval. Most banks will require her to come to the bank to sign the bank's documentation. If she wants to create an agency account with you as an authorized user, the two of you would need to go to the bank to open the account, and you'd both sign a signature card. You could also consider setting up a separate account into which enough money to pay the monthly bills is automatically transferred from her account.

A few banks offer monitoring accounts, which allow another trusted person to see the bank statements but not make transactions. The person you care for may be more willing to allow this type of account than other options. It might enable the trusted person to intervene perhaps before scammers do too much harm. Some banks might also notify both the customer and the financial caregiver if there are unusual transactions, such as a particularly large withdrawal. Such monitoring accounts may also avoid the need for a joint account, which can have disadvantages for both signatories, such as being sued for the debts of either person on the account, and raise tax and Medicaid issues. Joint accounts have also been used to facilitate financial exploitation because the other signatory can withdraw the money or use it for his or her own needs, not the other person's.

It's important to know special rules that apply to Social Security benefits and bank accounts. There should be a separate bank account just for those funds. That is because creditors cannot garnish Social Security benefits, but only if those funds are not mixed with money from other sources. If money from, for example, a garage sale or gifts from family members is added to that account, the money from Social Security loses its protection from bill collectors.

Another legal twist about Social Security payments is that only the beneficiary can spend that money. So, the Social Security payments should not go into a joint account with someone else, including a spouse or caregiver. If the beneficiary needs help managing that money, the caregiver should apply to Social Security to become the representative payee and then set up a special agency account. The account would be in the beneficiary's name and must show the representative payee's relationship. Examples of how to title the account are "(beneficiary's name) by (your name), representative payee" or "(your name), representative payee for (beneficiary's name)." The representative payee doesn't own the money, must spend it only on the beneficiary's needs, and must report annually to Social Security how the money was spent. Even if you are an agent with a power of attorney or court-appointed guardian, you must become a representative payee before you can manage any Social Security benefits. For more information about the representative payee's responsibilities, see Chapter 4.

✓   **Understand Social Security benefits and how to navigate the system**

If the person you care for receives Social Security, you'll need to understand how Social Security works to make sure she is taking full advantage of the benefits. If she is not yet receiving Social Security and is eligible, you'll want to apply for this benefit.

Before someone can receive monthly cash benefits, the individual must be credited for a certain amount of work under Social Security. For most benefits, the worker must have at least ten years of Social Security–covered employment. The number of credits someone must establish depends on the age of the worker and the type of benefit: retirement, survivor, or disability benefit. You can find details on specific requirements at www.ssa.gov or at any Social Security Administration (SSA) office located throughout the country. You can find those addresses at the SSA website or in your phone book.

When you go to the Social Security office to apply for available benefits, you will need to have the person's Social Security number along with copies of any marriage licenses, birth certificates, and other documents.

Be sure you understand the best time to begin receiving retirement benefits. People can start receiving retirement checks as early as age 62, but the amount is reduced up to 30 percent if benefits begin before full retirement age. For those born between 1943 and 1954, the full retirement age is 66. Waiting until age 70 to take Social Security retirement benefits increases the amount. Check out the chart at www.ssa.gov/pubs/ageincrease.htm for more details on how the benefit amount changes based on when benefits start. Keep in mind that a spouse will receive a significant reduction in the amount of survivor benefits if the worker starts taking retirement benefit early.

If the person you care for receives or is eligible to receive retirement or disability benefits, family members are also eligible for benefits under the following circumstances:

- Unmarried children under 18 (or 19 if a full-time elementary or secondary school student)
- Unmarried children 18 or older who were severely disabled before age 22 and who continue to be disabled
- A wife or husband 62 or older who has been married to the worker for at least one year
- A wife or husband under 62 if she or he is caring for a child under 16 (or disabled) who is receiving a benefit under the worker's earnings

A divorced spouse who has been divorced at least two years can receive benefits at age 62, regardless of whether the former spouse receives them. The marriage must have lasted ten years or more; the former spouse must be at least 62 and eligible for Social Security benefits, regardless of whether he or she has retired; and the divorced spouse must not be eligible for an equal or higher benefit on his or her own—or anyone else's—Social Security record.

For comprehensive information concerning Social Security benefits, see AARP's *Social Security for Dummies* by Jonathan Peterson (www.AARP.org/SS4Dummies).

✓ Check out veterans' benefits

The Department of Veterans Affairs (VA) is charged with administering benefits available to veterans who have served on active duty in the U.S. military service. The available benefits depend on the length of service, the time period during which the service was performed, whether the veteran was disabled, whether the disability was caused by active service, and many other criteria.

If the person you are caring for is a veteran, you'll want to access all available benefits. Under certain circumstances, the following benefits (and many more) may be available to veterans:

- Pensions for disability caused by service-connected injury or disease
- Pensions for certain non-service-connected disabilities
- Automobile allowance for service-connected loss or permanent loss of the use of one or both hands or feet
- Hospitalization benefits
- Help paying for the assistance of another in your home
- Alcohol and drug dependence treatment
- Nursing home care
- Outpatient medical treatment
- Prosthetic appliances
- Dental care
- Vocational rehabilitation and counseling
- Loan guaranty benefits
- Insurance
- Federal civil service preference

✓ Get a copy of military service records

You will need to have documentation of the veteran's military service to apply for any benefits available to the veteran or the veteran's family. You can get a copy of a service record (DD-214) at www.archives.gov/veterans/military-service-records/. Veterans can request their own military records, including medical records, by going online at www.archives.gov/veterans/military-service-records/evetrecs-help.html (eVetRecs). They need to include the veteran's complete name used while in service, service number, Social Security number, branch of service, dates of service, and date and place of birth. The veterans must sign and date the request and mail or fax it to the National Personnel Records Center (NPRC). The fax number is 314-801-9195. The mailing address for the NPRC is Military Personnel Records, 1 Archives Drive, St. Louis, MO 63138. The next of kin of a deceased veteran may also request military records using eVetRecs or by written application using Standard Form 180 and providing proof of death (death certificate, letter from a funeral

147

home, or published obituary). You may also need a copy of the veteran's marriage license, birth certificate, and children's birth certificates or adoption papers to apply for certain benefits.

✓ Apply for other available public benefits

Use the Public Benefits Checklist in this chapter to get an idea of the various programs that the person you care for may be eligible. Each of these programs has different eligibility requirements; take the time to check each one out. The tool at www.aarp.org/quicklink has explanations and applications for most public benefit programs in your area. To find services and programs for seniors in your community, use the Eldercare Locator at www.usa .gov/directory/federal/eldercare-locator.shtml.

✓ Look for outstanding loans and debts

On the positive side of the balance sheet, record any loans that are outstanding. Are payments being made? Can those who owe money pay it back? Record that information on the Outstanding Loans Checklist.

You'll also need to track down all debts, including credit card accounts. Most credit card accounts are a form of revolving credit. In general, that means the borrower is allowed to borrow up to a maximum amount with the expectation that there will be monthly or periodic payments to reduce the amount owed. As long as charges are kept below the maximum amount, new charges can be made. Also, as long as the amount borrowed is paid off in full the next month, no interest is due. As we all know, any amount not paid in full is going to be charged interest. If payments are late, penalties may also be due.

A wallet or billfold is an obvious place to start looking for credit cards. A check register or bank statement (paper or online) will give you clues about what credit card accounts are open. A credit report (from one of the three consumer credit reporting bureaus: Equifax, Experian, or TransUnion) will also list credit card accounts. Get free credit reports at www .annualcreditreport.com. Check there for accounts that may be open but inactive with no balance. It may not be difficult to miss most bills that are due. Notice of payments due on credit cards, utilities, mortgage payments, rent, phone—the sorts of bills that are routinely due—may quickly fill the mailbox. You should also check for statements or notices—as well as automatic online payments—that come via email.

In addition to credit card debt and other types of routine bills such as phone, electricity, and water, you need to find out if the person you're caring for has any other type of debts. She may have lent money to a relative or friend. You'll find out if there's any documentation of the terms of the personal loan so you know what needs to be paid. Other debt may be in the form of business loans, mortgages on other property besides the home, time-share fees, and condominium payments. You will need to gather all documentation of monthly payments and balances due to calculate the total amount of debt owed, deadlines for payments, and terms of the loans.

✓ Know how to deal with debt collectors

Although it's illegal, some debt collectors try to harass family members to pay the debts of other family members. The National Consumers League reports that "phantom debt" scams rose to fourth place of all complaints reported to www.fraud.org.

If you were not a joint owner of the credit card or any other type of debt, you are not responsible to pay the debt, even if the collection company says you must pay. Before promising to pay collectors or even sending any payment from your own account, you need to independently determine if you are in any way liable, if the amount they say you owe is even accurate, and if the time limit (statute of limitations) for having to pay anything has passed.

Debt collectors can be very persuasive and intimidating. They may lie about the amount due or your liability for the debt. They may threaten to harm your credit record and even try to sue you in court. These practices are against the law, but they happen. Debt collectors may be fishing for information about the loved one's finances or randomly calling family members in an attempt to find someone who can be talked into paying the debt.

If you get a call from debt collectors, take down notes of who is calling, the phone number and address, the collection company they represent, and all the details of the debt they are trying to collect (such as creditor, date on the account, amount, and names on the account). Never give out your personal information such as Social Security number, address, or bank account. Do not give out any information about other family members. The only question the debt collector can legitimately ask is who has legal authority to pay the debtor's bills. Do not answer any other questions, even if the caller sounds friendly or helpful. If the calls continue, have your lawyer write a letter demanding the collection efforts cease.

✓ Know how a reverse mortgage works

One possible source of money that could allow the person you care for to stay at home and pay caregiving expenses is a reverse mortgage. A reverse mortgage is a loan against a home that requires no repayment for as long as the homeowner lives there. It is offered by the U.S. Federal Housing Administration to homeowners age 62 or older. These federally insured and regulated loans are called Home Equity Conversion Mortgages (HECMs). They are different from other types of loans because the borrower does not make payments during the loan.

Eligible homeowners can get a reverse mortgage, like a traditional mortgage, from a private lender (such as a bank) that is secured by the equity in the house. Unlike a traditional mortgage that gets smaller as loan payments are made, however, the reverse mortgage typically gets larger over time. The reason the mortgage gets larger is that compound interest on the amount borrowed continues to increase the longer the loan is in place. Borrowers do not need to make payments until they die, move, or sell the home. Then the entire loan must be paid back.

The homeowner can select whether to receive the loan proceeds as a lump sum or as monthly disbursements. Depending on the circumstances and needs of the person you are caring for, a reverse mortgage may allow her to stay financially secure at home without worrying about a mortgage payment. But the homeowner has to have enough resources to pay the upkeep, maintenance, and taxes on the home.

Although the family may want to use a home's equity to meet caregiving or medical expenses, keep in mind that the up-front and ongoing costs involved in a reverse mortgage are high. These fees, including an origination fee, mortgage insurance premium, closing costs, and loan servicing fees, can amount to thousands of dollars. Unless there is a financial emergency, consider other options before taking out a reverse mortgage.

Because reverse mortgages are quite different from any other loan, do your homework carefully and thoroughly before considering one. As a protection to homeowners so they understand all the consequences and benefits of a reverse mortgage, they must receive independent counseling by a certified counselor before the lender can issue the loan. You can find a list of certified HECM counselors at https://entp.hud.gov/idapp/html/hecm_agency_look.cfm.

Money Matters Action Checklists

The following Action Checklists are included in Chapter 7:

- ❏ *Income*
- ❏ *Bank Accounts*
- ❏ *Social Security Benefits*
- ❏ *Veterans' Benefits*
- ❏ *Public Benefits*
- ❏ *Expenses*
- ❏ *Credit and Debit Cards*
- ❏ *Lawsuits and Judgments*
- ❏ *Outstanding Loans*
- ❏ *Personal Debts*
- ❏ *Reverse Mortgage*

Income

The person I care for has the following sources of income:

❑   Social Security

When received (monthly/quarterly/annually): _____

Deposited to account #: _____

Amount: $_____

❑   Pension

When received (monthly/quarterly/annually): _____

Deposited to account #: _____

Amount: $_____

❑   Veterans Administration

When received (monthly/quarterly/annually): _____

Deposited to account #: _____

Amount: $_____

❑   Retirement plan

When received (monthly/quarterly/annually): _____

Deposited to account #: _____

Amount: $_____

❑   Annuity

When received (monthly/quarterly/annually): _____

Deposited to account #: _____

Amount: $_____

❑ Long-term care insurance

When received (monthly/quarterly/annually): _____

Deposited to account #: _____

Amount: $_____

❑ Rental income

When received (monthly/quarterly/annually): _____

Deposited to account #: _____

Amount: $_____

❑ Family

When received (monthly/quarterly/annually): _____

Deposited to account #: _____

Amount: $_____

❑ Family

When received (monthly/quarterly/annually): _____

Deposited to account #: _____

Amount: $_____

❑ Other

When received (monthly/quarterly/annually): _____

Deposited to account #: _____

Amount: $_____

Bank Accounts

❑   The person I care for has the following checking or savings accounts at banks or credit unions:

NOTE OF CAUTION: Carefully secure this banking information.

Name of institution: _____

Phone: _____ Fax: _____

Address: _____

_____

Website: _____

Bank routing #: _____

Account #: _____

ATM PIN: _____

Online banking user ID: _____

Online banking password: _____

The account is

❑   In the name of _____

❑   Joint with right of survivorship with _____

❑   Agency or convenience account with _____

❑   Pay on death account with _____

❑   Monitoring account with _____

Name of institution: _____

Phone: _____ Fax: _____

Address: _____

_____

Website: _____

Bank routing #: _____

Account #: _____

ATM PIN: _____

Online banking user ID: _____

Online banking password: _____

The account is

❏ In the name of _____

❏ Joint with right of survivorship with _____

❏ Agency or convenience account with _____

❏ Pay on death account with _____

❏ Monitoring account with _____

Name of institution: _____

Phone: _____ Fax: _____

Address: _____

_____

Website: _____

Bank routing #: _____

Account #: _____

ATM PIN: _____

Online banking user ID: _____

Online banking password: _____

The account is

❏ In the name of _____

❏ Joint with right of survivorship with _____

❏ Agency or convenience account with _____

❏ Pay on death account with _____

❏ Monitoring account with _____

Name of institution: _____

Phone: _____ Fax: _____

Address: _____

_____

Website: _____

Bank routing #: _____

Account #: _____

ATM PIN: _____

Online banking user ID: _____

Online banking password: _____

The account is

❑ In the name of_____

❑ Joint with right of survivorship with _____

❑ Agency or convenience account with _____

❑ Pay on death account with _____

❑ Monitoring account with _____

Name of institution: _____

Phone: _____ Fax: _____

Address: _____

_____

Email: _____ Website: _____

Bank routing #: _____

Account #: _____

ATM PIN: _____

Online banking user ID: _____

Online banking password: _____

The account is

❑ In the name of_____

❑ Joint with right of survivorship with _____

❑ Agency or convenience account with _____

❑ Pay on death account with _____

❑ Monitoring account with _____

Social Security Benefits

- ❑ The person I care for is eligible for Social Security benefits.

- ❑ The person I care for receives monthly Social Security benefits.

- ❑ The person I care for worked in the railroad industry at any time after January 1, 1937 (which may affect the amount of Social Security received).

Name on Social Security card: _____

Social Security number: _____

Type of Social Security benefit: _____

(Disability, Retirement, Widow, etc.)

Monthly Social Security benefit amount: $ _____

Social Security benefit is deposited at _____ .

Veterans' Benefits

❑   The person I care for served in the U.S. military.

Full present name: _____

                          First   *Middle*   *Last*

Name served under: _____

                          First   *Middle*   *Last*

Military service number (DD-214): _____

Date entered active service: _____

Date separated from active service: _____

Service post-9/11: _____

Type of discharge: _____

Branch: _____

Grade or rank: _____

National Guard: _____

Reserves: _____

VA Medical Center: _____

Address: _____

Caregiver support coordinator: _____

Telephone: _____

Email: _____

Public Benefits

❑ The person I care for is eligible (or I will investigate eligibility) for the following public benefits:

❑ Earned income tax credit: Reduced taxes for low-income workers (www.irs .gov/Individuals/EITC-Home-Page-Its-easier-than-ever-to-find-out-if-you -qualify-for-EITC)

❑ Food benefits (SNAP): Help with grocery costs (www.fns.usda.gov/snap)

❑ Lifeline: Help with cost of telephone services (www.fcc.gov/guides /lifeline-and-link-affordable-telephone-service-income-eligible-consumers)

❑ Low Income Home Energy Assistance Program: Help with weatherization and heating and cooling costs (www.acf.hhs.gov/programs/ocs/programs/liheap)

❑ Medicaid: Help with medical expenses through local social services office (www.healthcare.gov/using-insurance/low-cost-care/medicaid)

❑ Medicare Part D Extra Help: Help with prescription drug costs (www .socialsecurity.gov/prescriptionhelp)

❑ Medicare savings plans: Help with Medicare premiums, co-pays, and deductibles (www.socialsecurity.gov/medicare/prescriptionhelp/cms.html)

❑ Social Security Disability: Income support for persons with disabilities (www .socialsecurity.gov/disabilityssi/)

❑ State pharmaceutical assistance programs: Help with prescription drug costs (www.medicare.gov/pharmaceutical-assistance-program/state-programs.aspx)

❑ State property tax relief: State programs to lower property taxes (www .lincolninst.edu/subcenters/significant-features-property-tax/Report _Residential_Property_Tax_Relief_Programs.aspx)

❑ Supplemental Security Income: Income support for persons who are over 65, blind, or disabled with very limited income (www.socialsecurity.gov /disabilityssi/ssi.html)

❑ Veterans' benefits: Benefits for veterans of the U.S. military service (www .va.gov)

Expenses

❏   The person I care for has the following expenses:

Item	Amount	On Autopay Yes No
Rent		
Mortgage		
Home repair		
Housekeeping		
Yard care		
Homeowner's insurance		
Household supplies		
Security system		
Medical alert		
Gas		
Electric		
Water/sewer		
Phone (land)		
Phone (mobile)		
Fuel oil		
Internet access		
Cable		
Medicare Part B premium		
Medicare Part D premium		
Medicare Advantage premium		
Medicare supplement premium		
Long-term care insurance premium		
Medications		
Medical co-payments/deductibles		
Home care/caregiver		

Car insurance		
Car repair/maintenance		
Car registration		
Parking		
Gasoline		
Taxes		
Credit card debt		
Groceries		
Entertainment		
Pet care		
Gifts		
Membership dues		
Subscriptions		
TOTAL MONTHLY EXPENSES		

Credit and Debit Cards

❑　The person I care for has the following credit or debit cards:

Name of credit card: _____

Contact phone: _____

Address: _____

_____

Account #: _____

PIN: _____

Amount due: _____

Name(s) on account: _____

　❑　Monthly payments are on autopay.

Name of credit card: _____

Contact phone: _____

Address: _____

_____

Account #: _____

PIN: _____

Amount due: _____

Name(s) on account: _____

　❑　Monthly payments are on autopay.

Name of credit card: _____

Contact phone: _____

Address: _____

_____

Account #: _____

PIN: _____

Amount due: _____

Name(s) on account: _____

　❑　Monthly payments are on autopay.

Name of credit card: _____

Contact phone: _____

Address: _____

_____

Account #: _____

PIN: _____

Amount due: _____

Name(s) on account: _____

❏   Monthly payments are on autopay.

Name of credit card: _____

Contact phone: _____

Address: _____

_____

Account #: _____

PIN: _____

Amount due: _____

Name(s) on account: _____

❏   Monthly payments are on autopay.

Name of credit card: _____

Contact phone: _____

Address: _____

_____

Account #: _____

PIN: _____

Amount due: _____

Name(s) on account: _____

❏   Monthly payments are on autopay.

Location of usernames and passwords for online access: _____

Lawsuits and Judgments

❑   The following lawsuits or legal claims are pending:

Case name: _____

Court: _____

Attorney: _____

Type of lawsuit or legal claim: _____

Case name: _____

Court: _____

Attorney: _____

Type of lawsuit or legal claim: _____

The following legal judgments are uncollected:

Case name: _____

Court: _____

Attorney: _____

Type of judgment: _____

Case name: _____

Court: _____

Attorney: _____

Type of judgment: _____

Outstanding Loans

❑   The following people owe money to the person I care for:

Name of borrower: _____

Contact phone: _____

Address: _____

_____

Amount due: _____

Name of borrower: _____

Contact phone: _____

Address: _____

_____

Amount due: _____

Name of borrower: _____

Contact phone: _____

Address: _____

_____

Amount due: _____

Personal Debts

❏ The person I care for owes the following people or entities money:

Internal Revenue Service: _____

Contact phone: _____

Address: _____

_____

Amount due: _____

Terms of debt: _____

State Department of Taxation: _____

Contact phone: _____

Address: _____

_____

Amount due: _____

Terms of debt: _____

Name of lender: _____

Contact phone: _____

Address: _____

_____

Amount due: _____

Terms of debt: _____

Name of lender: _____

Contact phone: _____

Address: _____

_____

Amount due: _____

Terms of debt: _____

Name of lender: _____

Contact phone: _____

Address: _____

_____

Amount due: _____

Terms of debt: _____

Name of lender: _____

Contact phone: _____

Address: _____

_____

Amount due: _____

Terms of debt: _____

© American Bar Association

Reverse Mortgage

❏   There is a reverse mortgage on the home:

Property address: _____

_____

Financial institution: _____

Phone: _____ Fax: _____

Address: _____

_____

Email: _____ Website: _____

Type of reverse mortgage: _____

Mortgage account #: _____

Current amount of debt: $ _____

CHAPTER 8

RETIREMENT PLANS AND INVESTMENTS

Knowing about money held in retirement plans and investment accounts will help you sort out how much money is there to pay for expenses. Money set aside during working years can be a primary source of funds to pay for daily living as well as care expenses. There may be pension income earned while working and savings put away in retirement plans such as 401(k) retirement accounts or individual retirement accounts (IRAs). Certificates of deposit (CDs) and savings bonds are other ways to invest, as are mutual funds, stocks, and bonds in brokerage accounts. Some investments and plans have special rules about when and how money can be withdrawn, with significant tax penalties for not doing it the right way. You'll need this information.

This chapter briefly covers some of the most common savings options and their unique characteristics. Rely on the advice of financial professionals for the specifics. Use the checklists as a convenient place to record information about retirement and investment accounts and contact information for brokers or financial advisers to ask questions. Chapter 2 has tips on how to select a financial professional.

My To-Do Checklist

Done	Need to Do	
❏	❏	Track down all pension benefits
❏	❏	Document all retirement plans and understand the withdrawal rules
❏	❏	Identify stocks, bonds, mutual funds, and other savings vehicles

✓ Track down all pension benefits

Although many employers no longer offer pensions, you should check with past employers of the person you're caring for—public and private—to determine if any payments are available.

Pensions are a way to accumulate tax-advantaged savings that can be tapped for a steady stream of income when the person you care for no longer works. Some pensions are financed entirely by the employer; others are co-financed by the employer and the employee. Pensions are considered to be ***defined benefit plans*** because employees receive a specific amount of money that is defined in the terms of the pension when they retire. To calculate how much an employee will receive, the plan uses a formula that includes the salary history and number of years the employee was eligible to receive pension benefits; this setup is called being vested in the pension. The retiree may, when she begins receiving the pension, have the option to elect if a surviving spouse will continue to receive a portion of the pension after she dies.

Talk with the pension fund manager at the company if you have questions about the details of any pension the person you care for is receiving to make sure she's getting all the payout she's entitled to.

✓ Document all retirement plans and understand the withdrawal rules

As you did for pensions, check whether the person you care for currently receives income from a 401(k), IRA, or any other retirement plan. If so, you'll want to understand the rules for withdrawal for each plan.

Many employers offer ***401(k) retirement plans*** that put off the need to pay taxes on both the contributions the employee and employer make and the plan's earnings until the employee withdraws funds from the plan, usually at retirement. People who withdraw money from their 401(k) before age 59½ have to pay a 10 percent penalty in addition to any income taxes. These 401(k) plans are called ***defined contribution*** plans. The employee makes a specific dollar contribution with each paycheck to a personal plan account. The plan invests the contributions (and the employer's, if any) in mutual funds or other investments that the employee selects from the plan's menu of investment choices. The plan account is credited with any returns on the investment.

Unlike fixed pension payments, the amount received depends on the performance (which may be positive or negative) of the investments. The employee may have the option, when she begins to withdraw money from the 401(k), to take a reduced payment so a surviving spouse can continue to receive a portion of the retirement funds after death, if the spouse outlives the employee.

You will also want to review any existing IRAs. The law, as of 2014, allows a person who is under age 50 and who has earned income to deposit up to $5,500 into an IRA account each year; for people over age 50, the amount is $6,500. Contributions to a ***traditional IRA*** may be wholly or partially tax deductible or nondeductible depending on whether the individual is also covered by a qualified pension plan or a 401(k), tax filing status, and income level. IRAs delay having to pay taxes on earnings from contributions until the individual starts to withdraw funds, usually upon retirement. Again, tax penalties apply to early withdrawals before age 59½, except in certain circumstances. ***Roth IRA*** contributions, on the other hand, are not deductible, but withdrawals are tax-free.

The person you care for may have other tax-deferred plans. These plans help defer taxes until the individual has reached an age when earnings have most likely begun to decline because of a lower income tax bracket. For example, if the person you care for was self-employed, he may have established a Keogh plan, which allows for larger, tax-deferred yearly contributions and greater benefits than does an IRA. A savings incentive match plan, known as a *SIMPLE IRA*, is a simplified plan, similar to a 401(k) plan, but with lower contribution limits and less costly administration. Another tax-deferred retirement for self-employed people is a simplified employee pension, or *SEP*, plan which is a type of IRA.

Because savings in retirement plans allow money to grow without paying any taxes, the tax laws require all those with retirement plans to start making withdrawals—and paying taxes—when they reach age 70½ or pay a penalty. These withdrawals are called required minimum distributions (RMDs). The RMD rules apply to all employer-sponsored retirement plans, including profit-sharing plans, 401(k) plans, 403(b) plans, and 457(b) plans. The RMD rules also apply to traditional IRAs and IRA-based plans such as SEPs and SIMPLE IRAs. The Internal Revenue Service (IRS) provides life expectancy tables and worksheets you can use to calculate the amount of any RMD at http://www.irs.gov/Retirement -Plans/Plan-Participant,-Employee/Retirement-Topics-Required-Minimum-Distributions -(RMDs). The tax penalties for failing to take the correct RMDs are a stiff 50 percent. The Roth IRA rules are different because you have paid taxes on the money you contributed.

Investors can start taking withdrawals without penalty at any time after age 59½ and can withdraw more than the required minimum amount.

✓ Identify stocks, bonds, mutual funds, and other savings vehicles

The person you care for may have various types of investments, such as stocks, mutual funds, or savings bonds. Of course, she's going to rely on her financial adviser for advice, but a quick overview of basic investments will help you understand what she has available to pay for care and other expenses.

Stocks

When investors own stock, they own part of a company. Companies sell these pieces of ownership, known as shares, to raise money to finance their business. By buying a stock, investors are basically betting that the company will grow. As the company does well, the stock generally increases in value. Investors can earn money on the investment when either the price of the stock rises or the company shares profits by paying a dividend. If the company does poorly, investors can lose some or all of the money they paid for the share.

The New York Stock Exchange lists more than 3,000 companies to invest in. Stocks are categorized in multiple ways: by industry (auto, biotechnology), market sector (utilities, health care), or geography (U.S., Asian), for example. They can also be categorized by size, as in large-capitalization, or large-cap (generally companies worth more than $5 billion), mid-cap ($1 billion to $5 billion), or small-cap ($250 million to $1 billion). Another way to group stocks is based on financial experts' perception of the company's basic financial health and historical performance. These categories include growth stocks, value stocks, and income stocks. Knowing how a particular company's stocks are categorized helps investors diversify their investments in different types of companies. Diversification reduces the risk of losing money.

Bonds

When investors buy a bond, they loan money to a company or government entity. The entity commits to paying the bondholder interest at a fixed rate for the life of the loan and to return the value of the loan by a certain date, called the maturity date. When investing in a bond, there's a risk that the company or entity may not be able to pay the interest or the principal. There is also the risk that if interest rates rise and the bond needs to be sold, the bond may lose value. That is because other investors can buy higher rate bonds, so the bond has to be sold at a lower price to attract a buyer. With *callable* bonds, the company has the right to buy back the bond back before the maturity date. This kind of buyback is normally done when the company can borrow at a cheaper rate.

Treasury Bills, Notes, and Bonds

Bonds issued by the federal government are the safest of all bonds. Treasury bills, notes, and bonds are available with maturities ranging from one to thirty years. The U.S. Treasury no longer issues paper Treasury bills, notes, and bonds. Those investments are managed online through www.treasurydirect.gov. They can be easily sold, but like all bonds their values rise and fall as interest rates change. There is no federal income tax on the interest earned. State and local governments also issue bonds—typically called municipal bonds, or "munis"—to pay for things like roads, schools, and public safety. Muni bond holders pay no federal income tax on the interest and may not have to pay state taxes if they live in the area where the bond is issued. Because of this tax advantage, the interest rates on governmental and municipal bonds are lower than on other types of bonds.

Mutual Funds

When investors buy shares of a mutual fund, they own a bit of various stocks, bonds, or other types of investments in the fund. Buying shares of a mutual fund helps diversify one's investments because the risk of losing money is spread among many different investments. Investments within a mutual fund are chosen by a professional manager based on the fund's investment objectives. The fund's objectives, set out in a public document called a prospectus, might be to own growth stock or government bonds, or invest in a particular industry, such as pharmaceuticals.

Morningstar, a provider of mutual fund research, tracks more than 15,000 mutual funds. Here are some of the common types of mutual funds:

- Stock funds that invest in the stocks of many companies
- Bond funds that are a collection of bonds purchased with pooled money from many investors

- Money market funds that include short-term, low-risk loans
- Balanced funds that include a mix of stocks and bonds
- Life-cycle funds, or target retirement date funds, that are designed to increase the percentage of bonds in relation to stocks as the investor gets closer to retirement age

Money market accounts and money market funds have significant differences. A *money market account* is a type of savings account available at banks and other financial institutions. Typically, the financial institution pays a higher rate of interest on a money market account than on a regular savings account. Account holders can make withdrawals at any time and can access the funds through automatic teller machine withdrawals or by writing checks. As with other accounts in banks insured by the Federal Deposit Insurance Corporation (FDIC), money in a money market account is insured up to $250,000. Account holders may have to maintain a minimum amount to avoid fees and be restricted on the number of monthly withdrawals. A *money market fund* is a type of mutual fund that is required by law to invest in low-risk, short-term debt. These funds are not insured by the FDIC.

Index funds or exchange-traded funds are similar investment funds to mutual funds. They try to replicate the performance of an index, such as the Standard & Poor's 500 index, by investing in all the securities in that index. This practice is called passive management, which results in lower management fees than mutual funds.

Savings Bonds

If the person you care for has invested in savings bonds, make a list of each bond, the type series (E, EE, H, HH, or I), denomination, and issue date. Depending on the type of savings bonds and their maturity dates, they may still be earning interest, or they may be just sitting at maturity and no longer growing in value. There is more than $15 billion in unredeemed bonds. The U.S. Treasury Department does not send out notices when bonds have reached maturity and stopped earning interest, but it is easy to find out.

Today savings bonds are redeemed and purchased online at www.TreasuryDirect.gov. Use the Treasury Hunt tool on the web at www.savingsbonds.gov/indiv/tools/tools_treasuryhunt .htm to find out how much each bond is worth today. The Treasury Hunt tool lists bonds that have reached final maturity and were issued after 1974. This site explains how to file claims for lost, stolen, destroyed, or undelivered bonds. Consider moving mature savings bonds that are no longer earning interest to a TreasuryDirect account where the proceeds will be deposited to a certificate of indebtedness. Find out more about how this works at Smart Exchange, www.treasurydirect.gov/indiv/research/indepth/smartexchangeinfo.htm.

CDs

Customers who use certificates of deposit agree to leave their money in the bank for a certain period—for example, two years—and during that time, funds may not be withdrawn without incurring significant interest penalties. In return for this long-term use of your money, banks generally pay a higher rate of interest than they would for savings accounts.

Factors that affect the interest earned include the bank's method of compounding interest and of crediting the funds in the account and debiting the money withdrawn. On the Certificates of Deposit Checklist, record any CDs, the bank where they are on deposit, and the maturity date to track when money can be withdrawn or rolled into a new CD.

Retirement Plans and Investments Action Checklists

The following Action Checklists are included in Chapter 8:

❏ *Pensions*

❏ *Retirement Plans*

❏ *Certificates of Deposit*

❏ *Money Market Funds*

❏ *Municipal Bonds*

❏ *Mutual Funds*

❏ *Savings Bonds*

❏ *Stocks and Bonds*

❏ *Treasury Bills, Notes, and Bonds*

Pensions

❑   I have checked with all previous employers to investigate possible pensions.

❑   The person I care for has the following pensions:

Employer: _____

Pension ID #: _____

Plan administrator: _____

Phone: _____ Fax: _____

Address: _____

_____

Email: _____ Website: _____

Pension amount: $ _____

Employer: _____

Pension ID #: _____

Plan administrator: _____

Phone: _____ Fax: _____

Address: _____

_____

Email: _____ Website: _____

Pension amount: $ _____

Employer: _____

Pension ID #: _____

Plan administrator: _____

Phone: _____ Fax: _____

Address: _____

Email: _____ Website: _____

Pension amount: $ _____

Retirement Plans

❏   The person I care for has the following individual retirement accounts (IRAs):

Financial institution holding the IRA: _____

IRA account #: _____

Phone: _____ Fax: _____

Address: _____

_____

Email: _____ Website: _____

Plan amount: $ _____

Financial institution holding the IRA: _____

IRA account #: _____

Phone: _____ Fax: _____

Address: _____

_____

Email: _____ Website: _____

Plan amount: $ _____

❏   The person I care for has the following 401(k) plans:

Financial institution/Plan administrator: _____

Account #:   _____

Phone: _____ Fax: _____

Address: _____

_____

Email: _____ Website: _____

401(k) amount: $ _____

❑ The person I care for has the following 403(b) plans:

Financial institution/Plan administrator: _____

Account #: _____

Phone: _____ Fax: _____

Address: _____

_____

Email: _____ Website: _____

Plan amount: $_____

❑ The person I care for has the following Keogh plan:

Financial institution/Plan administrator: _____

Account #: _____

Phone: _____ Fax: _____

Address: _____

_____

Email: _____ Website: _____

Plan amount: $_____

❑ The person I care for has the following SEP plan:

Financial institution/Plan administrator: _____

Account #: _____

Phone: _____ Fax: _____

Address: _____

_____

Email: _____ Website: _____

Plan amount: $_____

❏ The person I care for has the following Roth IRA:

Financial institution/Plan administrator: _____

Account #: _____

Phone: _____ Fax: _____

Address: _____

_____

Email: _____ Website: _____

Plan amount: $ _____

Certificates of Deposit

❏   The person I care for has the following certificates of deposit (CDs):

Name of institution: _____

Account #: _____

Maturity date: _____

Phone: _____ Fax: _____

Address: _____

_____

Email: _____ Website: _____

Account #: _____

Maturity date: _____

Name of institution: _____

Account #: _____

Maturity date: _____

Phone: _____ Fax: _____

Address: _____

_____

Email: _____ Website: _____

Name of institution: _____

Account #: _____

Maturity date: _____

Phone: _____ Fax: _____

Address: _____

_____

Email: _____ Website: _____

Money Market Funds

❑   The person I care for has the following money market funds:

Name of institution/Brokerage firm: _____

Account #: _____

Phone: _____ Fax: _____

Address: _____

_____

Email: _____ Website: _____

Name of institution/Brokerage firm: _____

Account #: _____

Phone: _____ Fax: _____

Address: _____

_____

Email: _____ Website: _____

Municipal Bonds

❏ The person I care for has the following municipal bonds:

Name of institution/Brokerage firm: _____

Account #: _____

Phone: _____ Fax: _____

Address: _____

_____

Email: _____ Website: _____

Name of institution/Brokerage firm: _____

Account #: _____

Phone: _____ Fax: _____

Address: _____

_____

Email: _____ Website: _____

Name of institution/Brokerage firm: _____

Account #: _____

Phone: _____ Fax: _____

Address: _____

_____

Email: _____ Website: _____

Mutual Funds

❑   The person I care for has the following mutual funds:

Name of institution/Brokerage firm: _____

Account #: _____

Phone: _____ Fax: _____

Address: _____

_____

Email: _____ Website: _____

Name of institution/Brokerage firm: _____

Account #: _____

Phone: _____ Fax: _____

Address: _____

_____

Email: _____ Website: _____

Name of institution/Brokerage firm: _____

Account #: _____

Phone: _____ Fax: _____

Address: _____

_____

Email: _____ Website: _____

Savings Bonds

❑   The person I care for has the following savings bonds:

Series	Denomination	Serial Number	Issue Date

Location of savings bonds: _____

Stocks and Bonds

❑   The person I care for has the following stocks, bonds, stock funds, or bond funds:

Name of institution/Brokerage firm: _____

Account #: _____

Phone: _____ Fax: _____

Address: _____

_____

Email: _____ Website: _____

Name of institution/Brokerage firm: _____

Account #: _____

Phone: _____ Fax: _____

Address: _____

_____

Email: _____ Website: _____

Name of institution/Brokerage firm: _____

Account #: _____

Phone: _____ Fax: _____

Address: _____

_____

Email: _____ Website: _____

Treasury Bills, Notes, and Bonds

❏ The person I care for has an Individual TreasuryDirect account:

Account name: _____

Password: _____

Account #: _____

❏ The person I care for has the following Treasury bills or bonds funds:

Name of institution/Brokerage firm: _____

Account #: _____

Phone: _____ Fax: _____

Address: _____

_____

Email: _____ Website: _____

Name of institution/Brokerage firm: _____

Account #: _____

Phone: _____ Fax: _____

Address: _____

_____

Email: _____ Website: _____

CHAPTER 9
TAKING CARE OF PROPERTY

In this chapter, you have an opportunity to take stock of all the real estate and personal property the person you care for owns and go over the ways it is, or can be, owned. Gathering this information is important for now and in the future, when decisions about where to live and how to meet expenses need to be made.

For many people, their home is the most important property they own. But they may have other property, too. Perhaps they live in a condominium where they own specific space in a larger property. They may own commercial property that produces income or they may own investment property they hope to sell for a profit. They could also have a time-share, where they have the right to access property for a limited time. The checklists in this chapter start the process of inventorying the various types of property the person you care for owns.

Because there are so many different ways people can own real property, it's important to understand the differences if owners are thinking of either selling or buying. They may be thinking about selling their home to downsize and move closer to grandchildren. Their plans may include buying a condo where it is warmer or investing in a time-share. Neighbors may have been talking about adding their children to the deed, and the person you care for wants to know if that's a good idea. How real estate is owned, or titled, makes a big difference. That's why in this chapter, you have an opportunity to take stock of all the real estate options and go over the ways it is, or can be, owned.

In legal-speak, property is divided into real and personal property. In addition to the checklists to inventory real property, there's also a checklist to inventory personal property. Obviously, not everything needs to be listed. While you are completing this checklist, you could also take photos or videos of family heirlooms or special possessions.

My To-Do Checklist

Done   **Need to Do**

❏	❏	List real property and review how it is titled
❏	❏	Discuss with a tax adviser or estate planner the pros and cons of adding a child to a deed
❏	❏	Determine if any property qualifies for tax relief
❏	❏	Consolidate all investment or commercial property records
❏	❏	Understand the terms of any rental agreements
❏	❏	Obtain a copy of the master deed and condominium association documents
❏	❏	Obtain and review any time-share contracts
❏	❏	Inventory special personal possessions

✓ List real property and review how it is titled

Whether the property is a single-family dwelling, business property, second home, condominium, or time-share, there are many different ways to own, or hold title to, it. Take, for example, all the ways to own a home. You can own it in your own name or jointly with others. You can keep the right to live in your home for as long as you live, even after giving or selling ownership to someone else (a life estate). Or you can put your home into a trust, which would then own it.

To make it even more interesting, there are ways to own or be able to use only part of the real estate. You can own the space where you live but not the building (condominium). Or you could rent an apartment, which gives you the right to occupy the unit. You could own the right to have access to a unit for a limited time (time-share). How the property is titled can make a big difference about what the owner can do with the property and what happens to the property after the owner's death.

As you go through this chapter's checklists, make sure you include how each property is titled. Look at the deed for words like "joint owners with right of survivorship" or "tenants by the entirety." Be sure to ask a lawyer to explain any deed or titling question.

Individual Ownership

People can own real property individually in their own name. In that case, the owner has the sole right to sell it, rent it, transfer it by will, and use it in any legal way. The owner is responsible for all taxes, maintenance, and insurance.

Property owners who hold real estate in their own name need to state in their will who they want to inherit this property. If they do not have a will, their state's law of ***intestacy*** will determine who gets it. Intestacy law sets up a priority scheme of inheritance. To a degree, it tries to anticipate who the typical person would want to inherit his or her property if the property owner had gotten around to writing a will. You should check to see what the state's priority scheme is, but typically real estate would first go to a spouse, and if no spouse, then to children; and if no children, then to parents; then to siblings; and so forth out multiple branches of the family tree to the closest living next of kin. Most intestacy laws also include rules of what to do when there are bumps in the family tree such as adopted children, deceased children with living children, or multiple marriages. Only if no living next of kin can be located does the state get your property, called *escheat*.

Joint Ownership

There are multiple ways to own real estate with someone else. The deed establishes whether there are joint owners or common owners. *Joint owners with right of survivorship* have equal ownership and rights to use and enjoy the property. All joint owners must agree to sell or mortgage the property. For couples who are not married, this type of property ownership ensures that the surviving partner will automatically inherit the property. Joint owners don't have to be spouses. If they are, some states call this type of ownership *tenants by the entireties*. When one of the joint owners dies, the surviving owner or owners automatically continue to own the property. The last surviving owner ends up as the sole owner of the property. This last owner can then leave that property by will to anyone he or she wants, or it will be distributed through intestacy rules. The owners are jointly responsible for all taxes, insurance, and maintenance.

Common Ownership

Ownership in common (called tenants in common) is the other primary way to own real estate with someone else. The key difference between ownership in common and joint ownership is what happens to the share of ownership when a common owner dies. Unlike joint ownership with right of survivorship, the surviving owner does not inherit any greater interest or share in the property. The common owner's share passes to the decedent's estate. Siblings who together own property, such as a beach house, may want to consider ownership in common so that each sibling's interest will pass down to their own children, rather than to the sibling or nieces and nephews. For example, Juanita and Louise as sisters share equal ownership in common of a cabin on a lake where their families frequently spend summers. Each sister has a will that states when she dies her property passes to her own children. When Juanita dies, Louise still owns half of the property, along with Juanita's kids who own the other half. The tenants in common share the upkeep expenses, or they can work out a division of costs.

Community Property

For spouses in nine states (Arizona, California, Idaho, Louisiana, Nevada, New Mexico, Texas, Washington, and Wisconsin), all property acquired during the marriage automatically becomes community property. The laws vary in each of these states, but the basic theory is that each spouse acquires an equal interest in the real estate. When a husband or wife dies, only half of the marital property can be inherited because the surviving spouse already owns his or her own right to half of the marital property. Each spouse has the right to assign by will the ownership of his or her portion of the community property. Property that either spouse brought into the marriage or inherits is considered separate property.

Trust Property

Another way to title property is to have it held in trust. Be sure to list all trust real estate in the Trust Checklist in this chapter.

The grantor of a trust is the person who creates the trust and deeds selected real estate into the trust. Although the grantor no longer "owns" the property (the trust does), the grantor determines who is to be the trustee to manage that property and when the trustee is to transfer that property to the beneficiaries. The beneficiary of a trust is the person who receives the benefit of the trust. When and how the trustee transfers title to the real estate to the beneficiary depends on the language in the trust document. As long as the property is in the trust, the trustee is responsible for maintaining the property, paying taxes, and keeping it insured.

Life Estate

By creating a life estate, the owner transfers the ownership of a home to another person, but keeps the right to continue living in the home until the original owner dies. Upon the original owner's death, the other person automatically gets the right to take possession. For example, Tom and Mary together own their home and want to remain there until the last one dies. They can create a joint life estate with their children as the remaindermen. Tom and Mary can live at home until the last spouse dies; then the kids own the whole property. The life tenants continue to be responsible for the taxes, insurance, and maintenance of the property, but are assured to live at home as long as they live. The remaindermen can sell their interest, but the new buyer has to honor the life tenants' right to continue to stay in place.

✓ Discuss with a tax adviser or estate planner the pros and cons of adding a child to a deed

Joint ownership with right of survivorship is typically the way spouses own their home because it is a convenient way to avoid the need to probate that property when the first spouse dies. That is because the surviving joint owner automatically becomes the sole owner on the death of the other owner. On the other hand, adding a child to a deed because the parents want the children to inherit their home is fraught with possible negative consequences, to both parents and children. Once the parents add a child to the deed they cannot sell the home, take out a home equity loan, or get a mortgage without the child's consent. They will not be able to get a reverse mortgage unless the child is also over age 62. If the child is sued, gets a divorce, or goes into bankruptcy, the jointly owned home will be involved in those legal entanglements.

By adding a child to a deed as a joint owner, the property owners are making a gift of the value of the home, which has tax and Medicaid complications. The owners may need to declare the gift to the IRS, by preparing gift tax returns. Refer to IRS Publication 559 at www.irs.gov/uac/Publication-559,-Survivors,-Executors,-and-Administrators for more details or consult with an attorney. Although it may at first sound attractive to the child that he or she is getting the house now rather than having to wait to inherit it, the different tax consequences between getting it now and waiting until later may make the idea less inviting.

When a parent makes a gift of a home by adding a child as a joint owner, the child gets the same basis as the parent had at the time the gift was made. *Basis* is important in determining the amount of taxes that will be due when the house is sold. As an example, Mary originally purchased her home for $250,000. It has increased in value to $400,000 at the time she makes the gift. She has made a gift worth $150,000. If the house is worth $500,000 when she dies, her heirs get what is called stepped-up basis, or the value of the house on the date of Mary's death.

Here's an example of how this would work: If her son *inherited* the home and later sells it for $600,000, he would have a basis of $500,000 and a gain of only $100,000. If the son was *gifted* the house, he would have a basis of $125,000 for the half he was gifted (half of the original basis of $250,000) and $250,000 on the half he inherited (half of the $500,000 value at date of death), for a total basis of $375,000. When he sells at $600,000, he has a gain of $225,000. At a 15 percent capital gains rate, the difference in tax liability is $15,000 versus $33,750.

Gifting ownership of a home may also prevent or delay homeowners from being eligible for Medicaid if they need to go into a nursing home. Medicaid rules consider that a gift made within five years of an application for Medicaid is a transfer for less than fair market value. It will assess an eligibility penalty that is calculated by dividing the value of the transfer by the state's average nursing facility private pay rate to determine how many months' wait before becoming eligible for Medicaid. Gifts can be made to a spouse without this penalty. Additionally, Medicaid does not include up to $500,000 of a home's value home in determining the maximum amount of resources someone can have to be Medicaid eligible.

Note: Tax laws and Medicaid eligibility rules frequently change and vary from state to state. Check with a lawyer experienced with taxation and your state's Medicaid rules before changing any deeds.

✓ Determine if any property qualifies for tax relief

Most states or counties offer some reduction in taxes based on the homeowner's age, income, disability, or military status. To find out about eligibility, contact the local office where the person you are caring for pays property taxes, state department of revenue or taxation, or local area agency on aging. To find out about special state tax policies available, check out the Lincoln Institute of Land Policy at www.lincolninst.edu/subcenters/significant -features-property-tax/Report_Residential_Property_Tax_Relief_Programs.aspx.

✓ Consolidate all investment or commercial property records

The people you care for may have a second home where they spend part of the year, land they inherited and share with other relatives, investment property that's rented out, or a farm operation that they run. As with any income-producing asset, help them maintain in logical order any records relating to the management of investment, commercial, or farm property. These records could include all business plans, land or equipment leases, rental income, easements, assessments, insurance policies, tax records, accounts payable, and inventories of all equipment. Understand the terms of any rental agreement and check with a lawyer if you have any questions.

✓ Understand the terms of any rental agreements

Renters may not own where they call "home," but they still have legal rights. Renters could live in an apartment in a retirement living complex, have a suite in an assisted living facility, or stay in a room in a skilled nursing facility. They could also have a contract with a continuing care retirement community, where the residents move from independent living to higher levels of services and care as their medical needs change while staying within the same campus or residential community.

The rights and obligations of those who live in an assisted living facility or other living arrangement where care services are available are spelled out in the resident agreement, including how long they can stay, how much to pay in rent, what services they'll get, and what to do when they want or need to move. Federal and state laws may regulate what terms can or cannot be in the agreements and set out residents' rights. Use the Assisted Living Facility Contracts Checklist and the Skilled Nursing Facility Contracts Checklist in Chapter 6 to know what to look for in these agreements. Be certain to have a lawyer review any contract you don't completely understand.

✓ Obtain a copy of the master deed and condominium association documents

If the people you care for own a condominium, you'll want to obtain a copy of the master deed and any association documents. A condo is a special form of ownership. Typically, a condominium owner individually owns a specific unit as well as jointly owns with all the other unit owners the common areas such as the public hallways, lobby, grounds, and recreational areas. The master deed, or declaration, describes the space they own, the common areas, and any restrictions on how they can use or modify the unit or the common areas. A copy of the master deed should be on file in the local courthouse.

It's also good to obtain a copy of the condominium association documents. The condominium association includes all the unit owners, who manage the condominium through an elected board of directors. The condominium association may also have a separate set of bylaws or rules that set out how the condominium is to be managed, pet restrictions, color choices, and how monthly unit fees are assessed, among many details.

✓ Obtain and review any time-share contracts

With a time-share, instead of owning property, you own the right to use property. With many time-share plans, multiple people have the right to use the same property, with each having a specific period of time when they have exclusive use of the property. The time-share may be for a specific week in a specific unit, for a rotating time schedule, or for part-time use of multiple properties. Because there are so many variations on the time-share concept, you'll need to have a lawyer review the contract with you to explain what happens to the time-share when a time-share holder wants to get out of the contract or dies.

A note of caution: It can be very difficult to resell some time-share properties. Because there are so many time-share options available, the resale value may be much lower than the purchase price and annual fees. The Federal Trade Commission (FTC) warns consumers who want to sell a time-share to ask a lot of questions of any reseller who promises a quick sale or says buyers are lined up to purchase the property. Before signing a contract with a reseller, make sure he or she is licensed in the state to sell real estate; check for any complaints filed with the state attorney general; and understand all fees, commission, and the length of the contract. Read the FTC tips on what should be in a resellers' contract at www.consumer.ftc.gov/articles/0073-timeshares-and-vacation-plans.

✓ Inventory special personal possessions

Now is a good time to inventory special possessions or assets of value. Make sure the list includes any furniture, paintings and artwork, coin or stamp collections, jewelry, and musical instruments that have great value. You don't need to list everything, but do include items of special interest or value. While you're at it, looks for receipts or appraisals. They are important in establishing the value of any special possessions. Having this inventory will make it much easier to file an insurance claim for loss or theft.

An additional way to make a record of personal property is to take photographs or videos as you walk through rooms, closets, cabinets, attics, garages, basements, and storage units. After you have documented these possessions, store the digital pictures or the video on a disk or thumb drive in a safe deposit box or other fireproof storage, or put them in cloud storage. You can indicate in this book where it is stored.

Then go the extra step to ask those you're caring for to tell any interesting stories about how they acquired special items. They could talk into an audio recorder or video camera, make notes by hand or on the computer, or dictate the stories to a family member. This is a good way to pass on the history of the silver bowl they got as a wedding present from Aunt Tully or how your mom haggled with a street merchant for the painting in the dining room. By capturing the stories now, future generations will know the opal ring came from your dad's maternal grandmother, and the pocket watch was Great Uncle Randolph's.

Taking Care of Property Action Checklists

The following Action Checklists are included in Chapter 9:

- ❏ *Commercial Property*
- ❏ *Condominium*
- ❏ *Investment Property*
- ❏ *Personal Property and Heirlooms*
- ❏ *Primary Residence*
- ❏ *Rental Residence*
- ❏ *Secondary Residence*
- ❏ *Time-Share*
- ❏ *Trust*

Commercial Property

❏ The person I care for owns the following commercial property:

Property address: _____

_____

Ownership interest:

❏ Sole

❏ Community property

❏ Joint with right of survivorship

❏ Tenant in common

❏ In trust

With: _____

_____

Purchase price: $ _____

❏ No money is due on the property.

❏ Money is due on the property as follows:

Financial institution/Loan servicer: _____

Phone: _____ Fax: _____

Address: _____

_____

Email: _____ Website: _____

Balance due: $ _____ Monthly payment: $ _____

Autopay:　　Yes　　No

Property address: _____

_____

Ownership interest:

    ❑   Sole

    ❑   Community property

    ❑   Joint with right of survivorship

    ❑   Tenant in common

    ❑   In trust

With: _____

_____

Purchase price: $ _____

    ❑   No money is due on the property.

    ❑   Money is due on the property as follows:

Financial institution/Loan servicer: _____

Phone: _____ Fax: _____

Address: _____

_____

Email: _____ Website: _____

Balance due: $ _____ Monthly payment: $ _____

Autopay: Yes   No

Condominium

❑   The person I care for owns the following condominium property:

Property address: _____

_____

Condominium association contact:

Name: _____

Phone: _____ Fax: _____

Address: _____

_____

Email: _____

Condominium association dues:

_____

Autopay: Yes   No

Purchase price: $ _____

❑   No money is due on the condominium.

❑   Money is due on the condominium as follows:

Financial institution/Mortgage servicer: _____

Phone: _____ Fax: _____

Address: _____

_____

Email: _____ Website: _____

Type of mortgage: _____

Balance due: $ _____ Monthly payment: $ _____

Autopay: Yes   No

Investment Property

❑   The person I care for owns the following investment property:

Property address: _____

_____

Ownership interest:

❑   Sole

❑   Community property

❑   Joint with right of survivorship

❑   Tenant in common

❑   In trust

With: _____

_____

Purchase price: $ _____

❑   No money is due on the real estate.

❑   Money is due on the real estate as follows:

Financial institution/Mortgage servicer: _____

Phone: _____ Fax: _____

Address: _____

_____

Email: _____ Website: _____

Type of loan: _____

Balance due: $ _____ Monthly payment: $ _____

Autopay: Yes   No

Personal Property and Heirlooms

❑ The person I care for has the following special possessions, including antiques, jewelry, art, furniture, silver, and musical instruments.

Item description: _____

Value: $ _____ Location: _____

Significance or history: _____

_____

_____

_____

Item description: _____

Value: $ _____ Location: _____

Significance or history: _____

_____

_____

_____

Item description: _____

Value: $ _____ Location: _____

Significance or history: _____

_____

_____

_____

Item description: _____

Value: $ _____ Location: _____

Significance or history: _____

_____

_____

_____

Item description: _____

Value: $ _____ Location: _____

Significance or history: _____

_____

_____

_____

Item description: _____

Value: $ _____ Location: _____

Significance or history: _____

_____

_____

_____

Item description: _____

Value: $ _____ Location: _____

Significance or history: _____

_____

_____

_____

Item description: _____

Value: $ _____ Location: _____

Significance or history: _____

_____

_____

_____

Item description: _____

Value: $ _____ Location: _____

Significance or history: _____

_____

_____

_____

Item description: _____

Value: $ _____ Location: _____

Significance or history: _____

_____

_____

_____

Item description: _____

Value: $ _____ Location: _____

Significance or history: _____

_____

_____

_____

Item description: _____

Value: $ _____ Location: _____

Significance or history: _____

_____

_____

_____

Item description: _____

Value: $ _____ Location: _____

Significance or history: _____

_____

_____

_____

Location of the letter of instruction on how and to whom these personal items are to be distributed: _____

_____

Location of photos or videos of these personal items: _____

Primary Residence

❑   The person I care for owns the following residence:

Property address: _____

_____

Ownership interest:

❑   Sole

❑   Community property

❑   Joint with right of survivorship

❑   Tenant in common

❑   In trust

With:

_____

_____

Purchase price: $ _____

❑   No money is due on the residence.

❑   Money is due on the residence as follows:

Financial institution/Mortgage servicer: _____

Phone: _____ Fax: _____

Address: _____

_____

Email: _____ Website: _____

Type of mortgage: _____

Balance due: $ _____ Monthly payment: $ _____

Autopay: Yes   No

Rental Residence

❑ The person I care for rents the following living space:

Property address: _____

_____

Unit: _____

Property manager:

Name: _____

Phone: _____ Fax: _____

Address: _____

_____

Email: _____ Website: _____

The person I care for can stay there until: _____

Monthly payment: $ _____

Additional payments for services: _____

Autopay: Yes   No

Secondary Residence

❑ The person I care for owns the following second residence:

Property address: _____

_____

Ownership interest:

❑ Sole

❑ Community property

❑ Joint with right of survivorship

❑ Tenant in common

❑ In trust

With: _____

_____

Purchase price: $ _____

❑ No money is due on this property.

❑ Money is due on this property as follows:

Financial institution/Mortgage servicer: _____

Phone: _____ Fax: _____

Address: _____

_____

Email: _____ Website: _____

Type of loan: _____

Balance due: $ _____ Monthly payment: $ _____

Autopay: Yes   No

Time-Share

❏ The person I care for owns the following time-share property:

Time-share management company contact: _____

Phone: _____ Fax: _____

Address: _____

_____

Email: _____ Website: _____

Type Share: _____ Purchase price: $ _____

❏ No money is due on the time-share.

❏ Money is due on the time-share as follows:

Financial institution/Mortgage servicer: _____

Phone: _____ Fax: _____

Address: _____

_____

Email: _____ Website: _____

Balance due: $ _____ Monthly payment: $ _____

Autopay: Yes   No

Annual maintenance fee: $ _____

Date maintenance fee is due:_____

It is payable to:

Name: _____

Phone: _____ Fax: _____

Address: _____

_____

Email: _____

Autopay: Yes   No

Trust

❏ A trust owns the following property:

Property address: _____

_____

❏ The person I care for is the grantor of the following property held in trust:

❏ The person I care for is the primary beneficiary of the following property held in trust:

❏ The person I care for is the secondary beneficiary of the following property held in trust:

Grantor: _____

Trustee: _____

Primary beneficiary/Beneficiaries: _____

Secondary beneficiary/Beneficiaries: _____

Property address: _____

_____

❏ The person I care for is the grantor of the following property held in trust:

❏ The person I care for is the primary beneficiary of the following property held in trust:

❏ The person I care for is the secondary beneficiary of the following property held in trust:

Grantor: _____

Trustee: _____

Primary beneficiary/Beneficiaries: _____

Secondary beneficiary/Beneficiaries: _____

© American Bar Association

CHAPTER 10

INSURANCE PROTECTION

The person you care for probably has various insurance policies: health, homeowner's or renter's, life, vehicle, and more. At this point, you'll want to track down and record them all to be able to file insurance claims, cancel certain policies, or obtain new ones to protect his property and health. You don't want to overlook any policies.

Insurance offers a way to spread the risk of financial loss among many people. With car or home insurance, for example, the payment of premiums protects the insured (to the limits of the policy) against losses from fire, theft, accident, or liability, depending on the type of insurance purchased. Any loss is shared by all those insured, saving the individual from possible financial disaster. The group, in other words, absorbs the individual's unexpected losses. Likewise, health insurance spreads the cost of health care among all policyholders. Many insurance companies offer additional liability protection through an *umbrella policy*, which provides insurance coverage in excess of regular automobile, personal liability, and other liability coverage. It can be a low-cost method of buying substantial protection.

Use the checklists in this chapter to record in one place all types of policies, with the names and contact information for the agents and companies, a reminder of when premiums are due, and where to file claims.

As you organize the various types of insurance, you may find policies that are no longer needed or that duplicate coverage. Or you could find that some type of insurance is missing. The following descriptions, although just an overview of the many types of insurance options available, should give you some information about the most widely used types of insurance coverage to help know what to keep and what might be discontinued. Be sure to have the person you care for consult with experts in this field.

My To-Do Checklist

Done	Need to Do	
❏	❏	Review life insurance policies and know how they work
❏	❏	Identify health insurance policies and know how they work
❏	❏	Verify or obtain homeowner's or renter's insurance

❏   ❏   Verify and keep updated vehicle insurance

❏   ❏   Identify annuities and know how they work

✓ Review life insurance policies and know how they work

You'll want to look for any life insurance policies owned by the person you care for. Although death comes to everyone and cannot be considered "unexpected" in the long run, it can certainly be unexpected when it occurs. Life insurance is a way to make sure surviving family members have cash to pay for final expenses such as medical bills or funeral. A life insurance policy can also be used to provide cash for any estate taxes or unpaid debts. It also may be important to provide the financial support the spouse, children, or other named beneficiaries depend on.

Today's life insurance market has multiple options to choose from, including how much coverage to purchase, the size of the premiums, how the policy is invested, any guarantees on returns, and how and when the policy proceeds are paid out to the beneficiaries.

A life insurance policy pays a designated sum of money to the person the policyholder named as the beneficiary to receive the policy proceeds upon the death of the insured person. The beneficiary can be the insured's estate or one or more individuals. This money may be paid in a lump sum, in a monthly sum for the life of another individual, in monthly sums over a certain length of time, or in some other manner spelled out by the terms of the policy. Regardless of the payment method for the premiums, the amount the beneficiaries will receive is set out in the policy. It may even pay double if the death is caused by an accident in what is known as a *double indemnity* policy.

Because of the many different types of insurance—*whole life*, *universal life*, *term*, or some other combination—be sure to get a detailed explanation of the benefits from the insurance agent. Depending on the policy and state laws, the person you care for may be able to borrow against the cash value of the policy. A very few states now allow policyholders to sell their life insurance policies at a discount to a third party to pay for nursing home care and remain eligible for Medicaid. These life insurance settlements come with a very deep discount, so it is important to discuss all the details of the transaction with an elder law attorney before the decision is made to "cash in" the policy.

✓ Identify health insurance policies and know how they work

If you are a caregiver, you are probably already familiar with any health insurance the person you care for carries. Most people get health insurance as an employee benefit where they work. Some people can continue to get health coverage through their former employer's health plan after they retire. Typically, with group health insurance, employees or retirees have an opportunity each year to modify their coverage.

Many different types of accident and illness insurance policies exist. Some are very limited in scope and pay out only if the policyholder develops a specific type of illness, such as cancer. Other policies, however, provide very broad coverage, although each has its limitations. At this point, you should locate all health insurance policies and understand what is and is not covered.

Medical expense reimbursement policies range from a policy that pays a fixed amount for each day of hospitalization to a health insurance policy that covers almost every medical expense that the policyholder could incur. Because the coverage varies to such a great extent, the cost of medical and accident coverage varies greatly. Be sure to review existing coverage and comparison shop for different coverage, if necessary.

Disability insurance is intended to provide financial stability if the policyholder should not be able to work because of an accident, injury, or illness. Some employers, unions, and professional associations provide disability insurance for their employees or members. Policies can vary in the amount of income that would be replaced, how long the payments are made, and what types of disabilities are needed to receive the benefits.

Health Insurance Marketplace

If you need to get insurance for someone who doesn't have health insurance and is not yet eligible for Medicare, you can shop for and purchase insurance in the Health Insurance Marketplace. Use www.healthcare.gov. The marketplace is a way to obtain health insurance that allows side-by-side comparison of the benefits and costs of approved health plans. All health plans sold in the marketplace must cover basic health benefits, including doctor visits, hospitalization, mental health services, and prescription drugs. People shopping for insurance in the marketplace can pick among several levels of coverage. Financial assistance to pay the premiums may be available, depending on income. Those who are eligible for insurance through a marketplace and do not buy it will be subject to a penalty.

Medicare

If the person you care for receives Medicare, you'll need to understand all the costs, the component parts, how the parts fit together for fuller coverage, and what to do if you need help figuring out Medicare claims.

Medicare is the federal health insurance program for people who are age 65 and over, for some younger people with disabilities, and for people with end-stage kidney disease. The Medicare program has several parts that provide different benefits. *Part A* helps pay for inpatient hospital care as well as preventive screenings, hospice care, and some home health care and limited skilled nursing care. Most people don't pay premiums for Part A coverage because they have already been paid for through payroll taxes. For those who need to purchase Part A, the monthly premium in 2015 is $407.

Part B helps pay for part of the costs for doctor visits, some home health care, medical equipment, preventive services, outpatient hospital care, rehabilitative therapy, laboratory tests, X-rays, mental health services, ambulance services, and blood transfusions. Those who turn age 65 are automatically signed up for Part A and Part B if they are receiving Social Security or Railroad Retirement benefits.

Medicare beneficiaries pay a premium for Part B. In 2015, the premium is $104.90 each month for people with income under $85,000 for an individual or $170,000 for a married couple filing jointly. People who earn more pay premiums between $146.90 and $335.70. The additional premium is based on the modified adjusted gross income reported on the income tax return filed the previous year. For example, the 2015 premium is based on the income tax return filed in 2014 for 2013 income. The premium is adjusted if income has decreased. For those taking Social Security, the Part B premium is automatically deducted from the monthly Social Security benefit. Those who are age 65 or older and not receiving Social Security can sign up for **Medicare Easy Pay** at www.cms.gov/medicare/cms -forms/cms-forms/downloads/sf5510english.pdf to have the Part B premiums automatically deducted from a bank account.

People can decide not to have Part B if they are covered by another policy. If their employer or retiree coverage ends, they have eight months to sign up for Part B. After that, they have to pay a penalty of 10 percent more in premiums for each 12-month period they could have had Part B but didn't sign up for it.

Part C is now known as Medicare Advantage. Medicare Advantage plans are offered by private companies. Purchasing Medicare Advantage coverage is an option. These policies pay for the same services as Parts A and B and may offer other benefits such as drug, dental, or vision coverage. In most Medicare Advantage plans, participants can go only to doctors, specialists, and hospitals that are on the plan's list of providers. During the annual Medicare open enrollment periods (between October and December), people already on Medicare can change Medicare Advantage plans or select original Medicare (Part A and Part B).

Part D helps pay for prescription drugs. Like Medicare Advantage plans, Part D is optional and offered through private insurance companies approved by Medicare. People already on Medicare Parts A and B can choose from many drug plans offered by many companies. The benefits and costs vary among insurance companies and each company's several plans. The first opportunity to elect to purchase Part D drug coverage is when newly eligible for Medicare; if you wait too long, there's a late enrollment penalty. Participants can switch to a different prescription drug plans or sign up for a Part D plan during the annual Medicare open enrollment period. Those with higher income (over $85,000 if single or $170,000 if married) will have to pay an additional $12.10 to $69.30 on top of the regular Part D premium.

As with most other insurance plans, there are an annual deductible, co-insurance, and co-payments for Medicare. Additionally, Medicare doesn't pay for all health care costs. It also does not pay for long-term care. To cover the gaps in Medicare, Medicare supplemental insurance, called Medigap insurance, is available. Medigap insurance covers some of the costs that Medicare does not pay, but not for long-term care. This private health insurance is offered by Medicare-approved insurance companies that can offer up to 11 standardized plans. Each standard plan offers a different set of benefits, fills different gaps in Medicare coverage, and varies in price. The standardization of plans makes it easier to compare policies among companies. A good reference on the intricacies of Medicare plans is *Medicare for Dummies* by Patricia Barry (www.aarp.org/MedicareForDummies).

Compare the various Medicare plans, including prescription drug, Medicare Advantage, and Medigap, at www.medicare.gov/find-a-plan. To sign up for Medicare, go to www .socialsecurity.gov/medicare/apply.html. To readily track Medicare claims and payments, sign up for a personal account at www.myMedicare.gov.

Those who need help paying the Part A deductible, co-insurance, and co-payments and Part B premiums and deductible can check out the Medicare Savings Programs. Depending on income, they may be eligible for Medicaid or may qualify for state programs that pay some of the premium or deductibles even if income and resources are higher than the state limits for Medicaid. A good place to get help understanding Medicare and Medicare Savings Programs is the local State Health Insurance Assistance Program (SHIP). To find the SHIP in your state, go to www.shiptacenter.org.

If the person you care for receives Medicare, pay close attention to the *Medicare Summary Notices* (MSN), which explain Medicare's action on claims that health care providers have filed. MSNs come by mail, or you can set up an account at www.MyMedicare.gov, where claims are posted within about a day of being processed. The MSN, which prominently says "This is not a bill," contains important information about the provider that filed a claim; the service provided; the amount Medicare paid; and the amount, if anything, the provider can bill the patient. If the patient has a Medigap plan that covers deductibles and co-payments, Medicare will automatically forward the claim notice to the plan for processing. For help understanding the information in a Part A or Part B MSN, go to www.aarp.org /decoders.

You should carefully compare all billing statement from the health care provider with the MSN to make sure the information matches: same provider, service or procedure, amount of claim, amount paid by Medicare, and amount the provider can bill. If, for example, a higher co-payment was made than Medicare calculated, contact the provider. If you see anything that doesn't look right, first contact the provider. It could be a simple mistake that the provider can correct. For bigger problems or suspected fraud, contact Medicare at 800-663-4227.

✓ Verify or obtain homeowner's or renter's insurance

Originally, fire insurance was about the only type of insurance that homeowners could obtain on their residence. Now they can get insurance to protect against windstorm, hail, flood, explosion, riot, smoke damage, and more. Insurance is also available for the contents of the home as well as a garage or any outbuildings.

Today, most homeowners purchase a homeowner's policy that combines fire insurance with extended insurance coverage that includes protection for personal property, additional living expenses if they can't live at home because of damage, and comprehensive personal liability coverage. This personal liability coverage would make medical payments to guests who get injured in the home and would pay for some damage to the property of others. Rather than having to purchase separate policies to cover each of these various risks, a homeowner's policy combines them into one policy. Similar types of policies are available to condominium owners and renters that cover personal property due to damage to the unit.

Riders can be added to the policy to fit specific needs or to insure special items such as antiques or jewelry.

✓ Verify and keep updated vehicle insurance

If the person you care for owns a car, truck, motorcycle, motorboat, snowmobile, or other vehicle, make sure that it is insured. In fact, most states require all drivers to be insured for liability to other persons for damages resulting from an accident. If a housekeeper or home health aide is going to be driving the car, check with the insurance company to make sure the other driver is insured in case there's an accident. The policy should include coverage for any person, family member or not, who has permission to drive the car. If other people are going to use the car routinely, it's good to add their names to the policy. Also be sure they have their own liability insurance and driver's license.

✓ Identify annuities and know how they work

Annuities are a type of insurance that are typically designed to provide a stream of income. As with other types of insurance, there are many types of annuities. They may be fixed, variable, or indexed, with immediate or deferred payments. Typically, money invested in the annuity grows tax-deferred, with payouts being taxed when received as return of principal and ordinary income.

If the person you care for invested in any annuities, payouts might be available to help pay for expenses. Investors have many options when setting up the annuity, including picking how the money is invested within the annuity, at what point the annuity begins to make payments, and for how long and to whom payments will be made. Payouts may be made for a fixed number of years, during the lifetime of the investor, or for the lifetime of a spouse or other beneficiary. Investors can also obtain, at additional cost, specific benefits, such as a guaranteed minimum death benefit or a guaranteed minimum withdrawal benefit. A guaranteed minimum death benefit, or GMDB rider, means that the beneficiaries or investor's estate will receive a set amount as defined in the GMDB contract if the investor dies before the annuity begins paying benefits. A guaranteed minimum withdrawal benefit, or GMWB, means that while living the investor receives a fixed percentage of the GMWB investment each year.

Insurance Protection
Action Checklists

The following Action Checklists are included in Chapter 10:

❑   *Health Insurance*

❑   *Homeowner's and Renter's Insurance*

❑   *Life Insurance*

❑   *Vehicle Insurance*

❑   *Annuities*

Health Insurance

❑ The person I care for has the following types of health insurance:

   ❑ Accidental death

   ❑ Dental

   ❑ Disability

   ❑ Hospitalization

   ❑ Long-term care

   ❑ Major medical

   ❑ Medicare

   ❑ Medicare Advantage

   ❑ Medicare Part D Prescription Drug Insurance

   ❑ Medicare Supplemental Insurance (Medigap)

   ❑ Surgical

   ❑ Travel

   ❑ Vision

   ❑ Other: _____

❑ The person I care for has health insurance with the following companies:

Insurance company: _____

Type of policy: _____

Policy #: _____

Group #: _____

Policy premium amount: $ _____

Premium due date: _____

Agent: _____

Phone: _____ Fax: _____

Address: _____

_____

Email: _____ Website: _____

Location of the policy: _____

Insurance company: _____

Type of policy: _____

Policy #: _____

Group #: _____

Policy premium amount: $ _____

Premium due date: _____

Agent: _____

Phone: _____ Fax: _____

Address: _____

_____

Email: _____ Website: _____

Location of the policy: _____

Insurance company: _____

Type of policy: _____

Policy #: _____

Group #: _____

Policy premium amount: $_____

Premium due date: _____

Agent: _____

Phone: _____ Fax: _____

Address: _____

_____

Email: _____ Website: _____

Location of the policy: _____

Insurance company: _____

Type of policy: _____

Policy #: _____

Group #: _____

Policy premium amount: $ _____

Premium due date: _____

Agent: _____

Phone: _____ Fax: _____

Address: _____

_____

Email: _____ Website: _____

Location of the policy: _____

Insurance company: _____

Type of policy: _____

Policy #: _____

Group #: _____

Policy premium amount: $ _____

Premium due date: _____

Agent: _____

Phone: _____ Fax: _____

Address: _____

_____

Email: _____ Website: _____

Location of the policy: _____

Insurance company: _____

Type of policy: _____

Policy #: _____

Group #: _____

Policy premium amount: $ _____

Premium due date: _____

Agent: _____

Phone: _____ Fax: _____

Address: _____

_____

Email: _____ Website: _____

Location of the policy: _____

Homeowner's and Renter's Insurance

❑ The person I care for has homeowner's, renter's, condominium, or second residence insurance policies with the following companies:

Insurance company: _____

Policy #: _____

Agent: _____

Phone: _____ Fax: _____

Address: _____

_____

Email: _____ Website: _____

Description of coverage:

_____

_____

_____

Monthly premium: $ _____

Location of the policy: _____

Insurance company: _____

Policy #: _____

Agent: _____

Phone: _____ Fax: _____

Address: _____

_____

Email: _____ Website: _____

Description of coverage:

_____

_____

_____

Monthly premium: $ _____

Location of the policy: _____

Life Insurance

❏   The person I care for has life insurance policies with the following companies:

Insurance company: _____

Agent: _____

Policy #: _____

Face amount: $ _____

Beneficiaries: _____

Phone: _____ Fax: _____

Address: _____

_____

Email: _____ Website: _____

Monthly premium: _____

Location of the policy: _____

Insurance company: _____

Policy #: _____

Face amount: $ _____

Beneficiaries: _____

Agent: _____

Phone: _____ Fax: _____

Address: _____

_____

Email: _____ Website: _____

Monthly premium: $ _____

Location of the policy: _____

Vehicle Insurance

❏ The person I care for has insurance for the following vehicles, including cars, air-planes, boats, motorcycles, and snowmobiles, with the following companies:

Vehicle: _____

Year purchased: _____ Purchase price: $ _____

Insurance company: _____

Agent: _____

Phone: _____ Fax: _____

Address: _____

_____

Email: _____ Website: _____

Policy #: _____

Policy premium amount: $ _____

Premium due date: _____

Location of the policy: _____

Drivers covered by the policy: _____

Vehicle: _____

Year purchased: _____ Purchase price: $ _____

Insurance company: _____

Agent: _____

Phone: _____ Fax: _____

Address: _____

_____

Email: _____ Website: _____

Policy #: _____

Policy premium amount: $ _____

Premium due date: _____

Location of the policy: _____

Drivers covered by the policy: _____

Annuities

❑   The person I care for has the following annuities with the following companies:

Insurance company: _____

Agent: _____

Phone: _____ Fax: _____

Address: _____

_____

Email: _____ Website: _____

Policy #: _____

Terms: _____

Beneficiaries: _____

Policy premium amount: $ _____

Premium due date: _____

Location of the policy: _____

Insurance company: _____

Agent: _____

Phone: _____ Fax: _____

Address: _____

_____

Email: _____ Website: _____

Policy #: _____

Terms: _____

Beneficiaries: _____

Policy premium amount: $ _____

Premium due date: _____

Location of the policy: _____

CHAPTER 11
MAKING FINAL ARRANGEMENTS

Whether a death comes suddenly or is anticipated after a long illness, it can bring a tidal wave of emotions. Some people may feel suspended in space and don't know how they will manage the next few hours, let alone the months or years to come. Many feel overwhelmed by the number of decisions that now must be made.

This chapter helps you prepare for that time. It looks at wishes about organ donation, cremation, autopsy, funeral service, and burial arrangements as well as plans for distribution of assets and personal property. Use the checklists to record advance plans that have been made, such as signing up on an organ donation registry, authorizing cremation, selecting a casket, discussing the funeral service with a religious leader or funeral director, and purchasing a burial plot.

If not all those plans have been made, use the checklists in this chapter as a way to start what may be difficult conversations. Some people may have very definite preferences and be glad you asked. Others may say they don't care. I've known for years that my husband wants to be cremated and the special places he wants his ashes scattered. As I was writing this chapter, I realized we hadn't talked about an autopsy, so I asked him. He's got an opinion on just about everything, but he surprised me with his response, "You do what you think is right at the time."

Knowing preferences ahead of time makes it much easier for family members to make the right choice when the time comes. They need to know that funeral arrangements have already been paid for at a specific funeral home and the location of the pre-need contract so they don't pay for funeral goods and services that have already been paid for. They'll want to be able to find any letter of instruction with details about plans for care after death. The Final Wishes Summary Checklist is an overview of the immediate decisions that need to be made. Use the other checklists in this chapter to note specific details.

My To-Do Checklist

Done	Need to Do	
❑	❑	Confirm wishes regarding organ or body donation and autopsy
❑	❑	Locate or support steps to create an ethical will
❑	❑	Know wishes for the body
❑	❑	Consider commemoration after death
❑	❑	Plan for burial
❑	❑	Check out burial benefits for veterans
❑	❑	Locate or support steps to create a will
❑	❑	Locate or support steps to create a letter of instruction

✓ Confirm wishes regarding organ or body donation and autopsy

Does the person you care for want to share the gift of organs or tissues with someone needing a transplant? It's often easy to find out. People can sign and carry an organ donation card. In many states, drivers can indicate their wish to be an organ donor on their driver's license.

Most, but not all, states have an organ donation registry. Find out at www.organdonor .gov/becomingdonor/stateregistries.html. For example, my home state of Virginia has a simple process to enter your driver's license number and some other identifying information at www.donatelifevirginia.org. On the site, you can indicate if you want to make a specific donation, perhaps of just eyes, or donate all organs or tissues that can be used.

If the person you care for hasn't decided yet, you can bring up the topic. Organ donations have saved or improved thousands of lives at absolutely no cost to the donor, yet there is always a very long list of patients waiting for organ transplants. According to the U.S. Department of Health and Human Services, 18 patients die each day because of the shortage of available donated organs. No one is too young or too old to donate organs; newborns and octogenarians have been donors.

Once the hospital determines that a patient who had just died wanted to make organs or tissues available for donation, doctors will examine the patient and determine if they are suitable for transplant. The organs or tissues are then removed through a surgical procedure. Most transplanted organs must be used within hours of the donation, while tissue donations of corneas, heart valves, skin, and bones can be preserved and stored in tissue banks. After the removal procedures, the body can be buried as though it were intact or cremated.

If the person you care for wants to make a ***whole body donation*** to a medical school or research facility, find out what the state's laws are. Some require that arrangements be made ahead of the death with the school or research entity. Find a list of anatomical research programs and learn more about what needs to be done to make these arrangements at www.med.ufl.edu/anatbd/usprograms.html. For example, the Virginia Department of Health has a state anatomical program where you can register your wish to make a whole body donation, download a Declaration of Intent form to give to family members and health care providers, and get information about what bodies cannot be donated and who in the family can consent if no Declaration of Intent is on file.

An *autopsy* is a surgical procedure used after a person has died to determine the cause of death. Autopsies can be done to further medical knowledge about a specific medical condition, such as an examination of the brain to confirm the specific type of dementia. A patient can give permission in advance for an autopsy to be performed for research or study purposes. Families need to consent to autopsies that are not required by law to be done. This procedure might also be done if there is a sudden, unexpected death. Clinical autopsies may be done when there are questions about the possibility of medical error, an uncertain diagnosis, or the proper course of treatment. And, of course, legal or forensic autopsies are done in criminal investigations when foul play is suspected, such as murder, poisoning, or suicide. These autopsies are done under the direction of a coroner or medical examiner, and no family consent is needed.

✓ Locate or support steps to create an ethical will

An ethical will may be one of the most cherished and meaningful gifts a person can leave behind. It's a way to share with family, friends, and future generations a person's values, blessings, life's lessons, hopes and dreams for the future, love, and forgiveness. Ethical wills are not new. They are an ancient tradition for passing on personal values, beliefs, blessings, and advice to future generations. Initially, ethical wills were transmitted orally. Over time, they evolved into written documents.

Preparing an ethical will can be an opportunity to put down on paper memories, insights, and special wisdom that shouldn't be lost or forgotten. For help getting started, find examples of ethical wills at ethicalwill.com/examples.html or www.personallegacyadvisors.com/knowledge-base/ethical-wills/contemporary-examples-of-ethical-wills/. Explore making a video or audio recording of the ethical will as a cherished legacy for later generations. The format doesn't matter. It could be in the form of a letter, thoughts written down over the years, a pamphlet, or a bound book created as a lasting legacy.

✓ Know wishes for the body

You as the caregiver and the family need to know what the person you care for wants done about his or her body after death. The options include being embalmed to delay decomposition of the body, a natural burial without embalming, burial in a coffin in a cemetery or in a crypt in a mausoleum, or cremation.

If the choice is cremation, the ashes may be buried in an urn at a cemetery, placed in a columbarium, or scattered. Those who wish to be cremated can forego being embalmed. With direct cremation, the body would go directly from the place of death to the crematory. Before cremation, an official will need to prepare a death certificate and obtain a cremation permit. Typically, a spouse or next of kin will need to sign a consent form before the body can be cremated. If cremation is the choice, talk about signing a pre-need authorization for cremation, especially if there is no spouse or close family. This document appoints the person the deceased wants to consent to cremation and to receive the ashes. A funeral home or crematory should have a form to sign ahead of time to ensure the wish to be cremated is carried out.

Every state has regulations concerning the scattering of ashes, so check with the state agency that regulates burials. The scattering of ashes at sea must be done at least three nautical miles from land, and the Environmental Protection Agency needs notice within 30 days of the burial.

More people are considering natural or "green" burials. With natural burial, the body would be promptly buried, without embalming, in the ground in a biodegradable coffin made of cardboard or bamboo, or in a shroud. A tree or shrub could be planted instead of having a stone grave marker, or a request could be made that instead of flowers, gifts be made to a favorite charity. On the Charities Checklist, list the favored charities and any information about where the donations should be sent.

✓ Consider commemoration after death

Do you know how the person you care for wants to be commemorated after death? Depending on family and cultural or religious traditions, she may want a funeral service at the cemetery or funeral home, a lively gathering of family and friends to celebrate her life, a memorial service, a viewing at a mortuary, a wake, a religious service in a place of worship, or no service or ceremony at all. Although there may be little difference in the service, a funeral generally means that the body of the deceased is present, while a memorial service is held after the body has been buried or cremated. If plans haven't been made, the person you care for may want to begin by talking with a faith leader or a funeral director.

It's a good idea to comparison shop for funeral goods and services. Funeral directors must give out written price lists with the costs for body preparation and transportation, caskets or urns, and grave liners or "outer burial containers." With the price lists in hand, comparison shop among several funeral homes to get the desired arrangements and have a better idea about the range of costs. Funeral homes can't require you to buy a casket from their selection; you can even shop for one online.

A funeral director can also help make arrangements for military honors and the type of grave marker or headstone. Headstones typically extend above the ground to identify the person buried. Grave markers lay flat on the ground. Some cemeteries or memorial parks require grave markers to make it easier to care for the grounds.

If there's a pre-need contract, understand what goods and services have been selected and the price paid. Review Chapter 6 on how to read a pre-need funeral contract.

Some people go so far as to plan all the details ahead of time, including the menu and the guest list. You can create a list of those who should be notified about the death on the

People to Contact Checklist. It will be handy to have in one place all the email addresses or phone numbers.

✓ Plan for burial

If the person you care for hasn't already done so, you may need to purchase a lot at a cemetery, a mausoleum, or a niche in a columbarium. The cost of cemetery lots or columbarium niches varies significantly depending on the location of the site. When purchasing a cemetery lot, ask about any additional charges for the opening and closing and perpetual care of the gravesite. Locate the deed or description of any cemetery plot or niche that has already been purchased. Be sure to record that information on the Burial Checklist or the Entombment Checklist. Also indicate on the Burial Checklist the desired inscription for the headstone or grave marker.

✓ Check out death benefits for veterans

If the person you care for is a U.S. veteran, family members may receive the following benefits at the time of death. The funeral director can help the family with the arrangements with the Department of Veterans Affairs (VA) to receive these benefits. Find out more at www.va.gov/survivors/ or request a copy of the *Federal Benefits Manual for Veterans and Dependents* from the local Department of Veterans Affairs office. On the Veterans' Burial Benefits Checklist, indicate which benefits the veteran wants.

Burial flag. A U.S. flag may be issued to drape over the casket of an eligible veteran. After the funeral service, the flag may be given to the next of kin or close friend or associate. Flags are issued at any VA office and most local post offices. A Presidential Memorial Certificate is also available at no cost to the family.

Burial in national cemeteries. Burial in a national cemetery is open to all members of the armed forces and veterans having met minimum active service duty requirements and having been discharged under conditions other than dishonorable. A spouse, widow or widower, minor children, and, under certain conditions, unmarried adult children are also eligible for burial in a national cemetery. In most cases, one gravesite and a single marker are provided for the burial of all eligible family members. When both spouses are veterans, you can request two gravesites and two headstones or markers. Certain members of the armed forces reserve components may also be eligible for burial depending on the space available. There is no charge for the grave plot, its opening and closing, a grave liner, or perpetual care.

Headstones or markers. The VA will furnish a government headstone or marker to be placed at a veteran's grave at any cemetery around the world. Even if the grave was previously marked, the family can obtain a government headstone. This service is provided for eligible veterans whether they are buried in a national cemetery or elsewhere. A headstone or marker is automatically furnished if burial is in a national cemetery. Otherwise, the family must apply to the VA. The VA will ship the headstone or marker, without charge, to the person or firm designated on the application. The VA will also furnish, on request, a medallion to place on an existing headstone or marker that indicates that the person was a veteran. The family must pay the cost of setting the headstone or marker, or attaching the medallion.

Military honors. By law, every eligible veteran may receive a military funeral honors ceremony, to include folding and presenting the U.S. burial flag and the playing of "Taps." A military funeral honors detail consists of two or more uniformed military persons, with at least one being a member of the veteran's branch of the armed forces.

The Department of Defense program "Honoring Those Who Served" calls for funeral directors to request military funeral honors on behalf of the family. Veterans' organizations may assist in providing military funeral honors. VA national cemetery staff can help coordinate military funeral honors at a national or private cemetery. For more information, go to www.cem.va.gov/military_funeral_honors.asp

Reimbursement of burial expenses. The VA is authorized to pay an allowance toward the funeral and burial expenses for eligible veterans. If it was a service-related death, the VA will pay up to $2,000 toward burial expenses. For veterans to be buried in a VA national cemetery, some or all of the cost of transporting the body to the cemetery may be reimbursed. If the death was not service-related, the VA will pay up to $300 toward burial and funeral expenses and a $300 plot-interment allowance. If the death happens while in a VA hospital or under VA contracted nursing home care, some or all of the costs for transporting the remains may be reimbursed.

✓ Locate or support steps to create a will

Does the person you care for have a will?

A will, or last will and testament, is the legal document by which "testators" determine who they want to receive their property after their death. In a will, the testator can leave assets to friends or significant others who are not related or make sure someone (other than a spouse) who would inherit if there is no will does not. Wills can also be used to make bequests to charities.

A will also names the person the testator wants to be the executor of her estate. It can name the guardian of any minor children until they reach the age of majority. If the will leaves assets to any minors, such as children or grandchildren, it may provide for the creation of a testamentary trust so their inheritance can be managed until they reach majority. A testamentary trust, unlike a living trust, is set up as part of a will and comes into effect after the death of the testator. The testator may also make donations or bequests to favorite charities, schools, or religious groups and take advantage of tax laws that encourage private philanthropy.

Ideally, everyone who has prepared a will has let someone in the family know where it is located. A word of caution: In most states, only the signed original will can be probated; copies will not be accepted. Similarly, strike-outs, erasures, and any other markings on the will can have the devious effect of invalidating all of it. A ***codicil*** is an amendment to the will that changes specific sections of the will. To be valid, it must be executed with the same formality, number of witnesses, and notary requirements as the original will.

Those who do not have a will can use the Will and Codicil Checklist to think through what they need to consider. Who should be the executor? How should property be divided? Should some property be in a trust? A lawyer can draft any necessary legal document. Review the tips on finding a lawyer in Chapter 2.

✓ Locate or support steps to create a letter of instruction

A letter of instruction is an informal document that serves as guidance to family members about matters they must attend to after a death. It can be attached to the will but is not an official part of it. Although it doesn't carry the legal weight of a will and is in no way a substitute for one, a letter of instruction clarifies any special requests for the family to carry out. Think of it as a flexible, informal supplement to the will that covers information more personal than what is typically included in a will.

A letter of instruction can have two parts that do two different things. The first part helps the family know how to find the information necessary to plan the funeral. The letter might include instructions about the type of funeral or memorial service desired, who should officiate, who should be asked to be pall bearers, or what songs should—or should not—be sung. The letter should tell about plans that have already been made with the funeral home of choice and whether any of the funeral arrangements have already been paid for. It could include a description of the location of any pre-purchased burial plot or crypt and where the plot deed is located. It may state directions for cremation and where to place the ashes.

The other part of a letter of instruction may help eliminate family feuds over who should receive specific personal items. We all have heard stories of family fights erupting over how to divide family pictures, necklaces, the stamp collection, fishing tackle, that figurine, or the wedding gift from Aunt Sue. The items may not have monetary value, but getting them to the right person can make a big difference to the whole family. Upon death, if the letter of instruction includes directions on how personal items are to be distributed, be sure those wishes are faithfully carried out.

Making Final Arrangements Action Checklists

The following Action Checklists are included in Chapter 11:

❑ *Final Wishes Summary*

❑ *Burial*

❑ *Celebration of Life*

❑ *Charities*

❑ *Cremation*

❑ *Entombment*

❑ *Ethical Will*

❑ *Funeral/Memorial Service*

❑ *Letter of Instruction*

❑ *Obituary*

❑ *Organ and Tissue Donation*

❑ *People to Contact*

❑ *Will and Codicil*

❑ *Veterans' Burial Benefits*

Final Wishes Summary

The person I care for wishes to:

- ❏ Donate organs and tissues (see the Organ and Tissue Donation Checklist)
- ❏ Donate the body to a medical school or research center (see the Organ and Tissue Donation Checklist)
- ❏ Be embalmed (see the Funeral/Memorial Service Checklist)
- ❏ Be buried in the earth (see the Burial Checklist)
- ❏ Be entombed in a mausoleum (see the Entombment Checklist)
- ❏ Be cremated (see the Cremation Checklist)
- ❏ Other: _____

The person I care for wishes to have:

- ❏ No commemorative service
- ❏ Funeral service (see the Funeral/Memorial Service Checklist)
- ❏ Memorial service (see the Funeral/Memorial Service Checklist)
- ❏ Celebration of life service (see the Celebration of Life Checklist)
- ❏ Graveside service (see the Funeral/Memorial Service Checklist)
- ❏ U.S. flag covering the coffin (see the Veterans' Burial Benefits Checklist)
- ❏ Military funeral honors (see the Veterans' Burial Benefits Checklist)
- ❏ Other: _____

Burial

- ❏ The person I care for wishes to be buried.
- ❏ The person I care for has a cemetery lot.

The ownership of the cemetery lot is in the name of _____.

Location of the lot:

Cemetery: _____

Section: _____ Lot: _____

Address: _____

_____

Other description:

_____

_____

Location of deed: _____

- ❏ The person I care for would like to have a grave marker.
- ❏ The person I care for would like to have a grave marker furnished by the Department of Veterans Affairs.
- ❏ The person I care for would like to have a service medallion furnished by the Department of Veterans Affairs.

The following words should be placed on the grave marker:

_____

_____

_____

_____

Celebration of Life

❑ The person I care for wants the following arrangements for a celebration of life ceremony:

Type of celebration: _____

Arrangement details:

Place: _____

Time: _____

Food or beverage suggestions:

_____

_____

_____

_____

Entertainment or music suggestions:

_____

_____

_____

People to invite:

_____

_____

_____

_____

_____

_____

_____

_____

_____

© American Bar Association

Charities

❏ The person I care for requests memorial donations or gifts be made to the following charities:

Charity name: _____

Contact information: _____

_____

Website: _____

Significance: _____

Charity name: _____

Contact information: _____

_____

Website: _____

Significance: _____

Charity name: _____

Contact information: _____

_____

Website: _____

Significance: _____

Charity name: _____

Contact information: _____

_____

Website: _____

Significance: _____

Charity name: _____

Contact information: _____

_____

Website: _____

Significance: _____

Cremation

❑ The person I care for wants to be cremated.

Following cremation, the ashes should be distributed as follows:

❑ Scattered in the following places:

_____

❑ Placed in an urn and buried or entombed:

_____

❑ Other:

_____

The following prearrangements for cremation have been made:

Company: _____

Address: _____

_____

Phone: _____ Website: _____

The contract is located: _____

Entombment

❑   The person I care for wants to be entombed.

❑   The person I care for owns a crypt, mausoleum, or columbarium.

The ownership of the crypt is in the name of _____.

Location of the crypt:

Church/Cemetery/Mausoleum: _____

Address: _____

_____

Space #: _____

Other description:

_____

_____

Location of deed or contract: _____

The following words should be placed on the crypt:

_____

_____

_____

_____

Other instructions:

_____

_____

_____

_____

Ethical Will

❏   The person I care for has created an ethical will or other legacy documents.

Ethical will:

_____

_____

_____

Books:

_____

_____

_____

Pamphlets:

_____

_____

_____

Videos:

_____

_____

_____

Other:

_____

_____

_____

Instructions for distribution:

_____

_____

_____

_____

_____

_____

_____

_____

_____

Funeral/Memorial Service

- ❏ The person I care for wants a funeral.
- ❏ The person I care for wants a memorial service.
- ❏ The person I care for wants a graveside service.

The commemorative service is for

- ❏ Friends and relatives
- ❏ Private
- ❏ Other: _____

The graveside service is for

- ❏ Friends and relatives
- ❏ Private
- ❏ Other: _____

The casket should be

- ❏ Closed
- ❏ Open

The urn with ashes should be present:　　Yes　　No

Location of the service:

Funeral establishment: _____

Address: _____

_____

Phone: _____ Email: _____

House of worship:

_____

_____

_____

Religious leader/Officiate/Clergy:

_____

_____

_____

Speakers/Readers:

_____

_____

_____

_____

Ushers/Pallbearers:

_____

_____

_____

_____

Favorite scripture, psalms, poems, readings:

_____

_____

_____

_____

_____

Special hymns, music, musicians, soloists:

_____

_____

_____

_____

_____

Letter of Instruction

❑ The person I care for has a letter of instruction.

Location of the letter of instruction: _____

Date the letter of instruction was last updated: _____

❑ The letter of instruction contains directions about the distribution of personal possessions.

❑ The letter of instruction contains directions about the funeral or memorial service.

❑ The letter of instruction contains directions about _____ .

Obituary

- ❏ The person I care for has not written an obituary.
- ❏ The person I care for has written the obituary.

Location of the obituary: _____

The obituary should appear in the following places:

Newspaper name: _____

Newspaper website: _____

Newspaper name: _____

Newspaper website: _____

Newspaper name: _____

Newspaper website: _____

On the following social media or web sites: _____

The following information should appear in the obituary:

_____

_____

_____

_____

_____

_____

_____

_____

_____

_____

_____

_____

_____

Organ and Tissue Donation

- ❑ The person I care for wants to donate any needed organs or tissues.
- ❑ Blood type: _____ .
- ❑ The person I care for wants to donate only the following organs or tissues:

Organs:
- ❑ Heart
- ❑ Kidneys
- ❑ Liver
- ❑ Lungs
- ❑ Pancreas
- ❑ Other: _____

Tissues:
- ❑ Blood vessels
- ❑ Bone
- ❑ Cartilage
- ❑ Corneas
- ❑ Heart valves
- ❑ Inner ear
- ❑ Intestines
- ❑ Skin
- ❑ Other: _____

- ❑ Location of uniform donor card: _____ .
- ❑ Wishes about organ donation are registered at this website: _____

_____

- ❑ The person I care for has given permission for an autopsy.

People to Contact

❏   The following people should be informed of the death:

Name: _____

Relationship: _____

Phone: _____ Email: _____

Address: _____

_____

Name: _____

Relationship: _____

Phone: _____ Email: _____

Address: _____

_____

Name: _____

Relationship: _____

Phone: _____ Email: _____

Address: _____

_____

Name: _____

Relationship: _____

Phone: _____ Email: _____

Address: _____

_____

Name: _____

Relationship: _____

Phone: _____ Email: _____

Address: _____

_____

Name: _____

Relationship: _____

Phone: _____ Email: _____

Address: _____

_____

Name: _____

Relationship: _____

Phone: _____ Email: _____

Address: _____

_____

Name: _____

Relationship: _____

Phone: _____ Email: _____

Address: _____

_____

Name: _____

Relationship: _____

Phone: _____ Email: _____

Address: _____

_____

Name: _____

Relationship: _____

Phone: _____ Email: _____

Address: _____

_____

Will and Codicil

❑   The person I care for has a will.

Drafting lawyer's name: _____

Phone: _____ Email: _____

Address: _____

_____

Executor's name: _____

Phone: _____ Email: _____

Address: _____

_____

Witness's name: _____

Phone: _____ Email: _____

Address: _____

_____

Witness's name: _____

Phone: _____ Email: _____

Address: _____

_____

❑   I have located the following codicil:

Codicil date: _____

Drafting lawyer's name: _____

Phone: _____ Email: _____

Address: _____

_____

Witness's name: _____

Phone: _____ Email: _____

Address: _____

_____

Witness's name: _____

Phone: _____ Email: _____

Address: _____

_____

Location of will and any codicils: _____

- ❏ The person I care for does not have a will and is taking the following steps to create one:
    - ❏ Inventory all assets and possessions
    - ❏ Identify how all real property, bank accounts, and financial accounts are titled
    - ❏ Review the designation of beneficiaries on all life insurance and investment or retirement accounts
    - ❏ Decide how assets are divided and who gets what
    - ❏ Determine charitable gifts to be given
    - ❏ Decide how and to whom personal possessions will be distributed
    - ❏ Create a Letter of Instruction for the distributions of personal possessions
    - ❏ Determine who you want to take care of your minor children
    - ❏ Determine who will manage the money any minors would inherit
    - ❏ Identify who to serve as executor and successor executor
    - ❏ Discuss expectations and responsibilities with potential executors
    - ❏ Discuss decisions with those named in the will

Veterans' Burial Benefits

- ❏ The person I care for served in the U.S. military.
- ❏ The person I care for wants a burial flag for the casket.
- ❏ The person I care for wants burial in a national cemetery.
- ❏ The person I care for wants a veteran's headstone.
- ❏ The person I care for wants military honors at the burial.

Name served under while in the military:

_____

          First   *Middle*   *Last*

Location of DD-214: _____

Date entered active service: _____

Date separated from active service: _____

Branch: _____

Grade or rank: _____

National Guard: _____

Reserves: _____